{ } human rights *first*

I0158158

Tortured Justice

Using Coerced Evidence to Prosecute Terrorist Suspects

April 2008

Table of Contents

About Us

Human Rights First believes that building respect for human rights and the rule of law will help ensure the dignity to which every individual is entitled and will stem tyranny, extremism, intolerance, and violence.

Human Rights First protects people at risk: refugees who flee persecution, victims of crimes against humanity or other mass human rights violations, victims of discrimination, those whose rights are eroded in the name of national security, and human rights advocates who are targeted for defending the rights of others. These groups are often the first victims of societal instability and breakdown; their treatment is a harbinger of wider-scale repression. Human Rights First works to prevent violations against these groups and to seek justice and accountability for violations against them.

Human Rights First is practical and effective. We advocate for change at the highest levels of national and international policymaking. We seek justice through the courts. We raise awareness and understanding through the media. We build coalitions among those with divergent views. And we mobilize people to act.

Human Rights First is a non-profit, nonpartisan international human rights organization based in New York and Washington D.C. To maintain our independence, we accept no government funding.

Acknowledgements

This report was written by Deborah Colson, senior associate, Human Rights First Law and Security Program, and Avi Cover, former senior counsel, Human Rights First Law and Security Program.

Editorial suggestions by Elisa Massimino, Kevin Lanigan, Gabor Rona, Devon Chaffee, Sahr MuhammedAlly, and Hina Shamsi, and the assistance of Melissa Koven, Sofia Rahman, Reagan Kuhn, Elizabeth Shutkin, Mariam Muzaffar, Allison Johnson, Laura Smith, Lauren Smith, and Aaron Hall, are greatly appreciated.

Human Rights First gratefully acknowledges the generous support of The Atlantic Philanthropies, JEHT Foundation, John Merck Fund, Open Society Institute, and The Overbrook Foundation.

This report is available for free online at www.humanrightsfirst.org

© 2008 Human Rights First. All Rights Reserved.

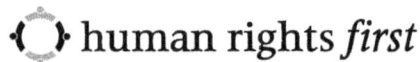

( ) human rights *first*

Headquarters

333 Seventh Avenue
13th Floor
New York, NY 10001-5108

Tel.: 212.845.5200
Fax: 212.845.5299

www.humanrightsfirst.org

Washington D.C. Office

100 Maryland Avenue, NE
Suite 500
Washington, DC 20002-5625

Tel: 202.547.5692
Fax: 202.543.5999

Introduction

"We have shaken the belief the world had in America's justice system by keeping a place like Guantánamo open and creating things like the military commission. We don't need it and it's causing us far more damage than any good we get for it."

— Former Secretary of State Colin Powell (General, U.S. Army, Ret., and former Chairman, Joint Chiefs of Staff), Reuters, June 10, 2007

"We can't measure the accuracy of this program by saying we've gone out and brought hard and fast cases based on it. You cannot tell me whether any of these individuals or all of these individuals have lied. You conceded to me that someone facing extreme anxiety and pressure could yield false information. I add all that up and I come to one simple conclusion: We can't tell if this program is working...[W]e want to get the real terrorists and we don't know if you are succeeding in doing that or if you're unearthing a bunch of lies."

— Representative Artur Davis (D-AL), House Judiciary Subcommittee Hearing on the Justice Department's Office of Legal Counsel, February 14, 2008, responding to Assistant Attorney General Steven Bradbury's description of the CIA's interrogation program

For years, the Bush Administration justified its reliance on military commissions as a means of expediting the prosecution of terrorist suspects. *"As soon as Congress acts* to authorize the military commissions I have proposed," said President George W. Bush in September 2006, "the men our intelligence officials believe orchestrated the deaths of nearly 3,000 Americans on September the 11th 2001, can face justice."[1] In fact, just the opposite has occurred. More than six years after the first men were brought to Guantánamo Bay, prosecutors have sought charges against just fifteen men and convicted only one.

Challenges to the lawfulness of the system itself caused much of the initial delay. In 2006, the U.S. Supreme Court struck down the first military commission system, created by the Bush Administration, on the grounds that it violated military law and the Geneva Conventions. The

administration's approval of secret detention and torture and other cruel interrogation techniques have posed additional obstacles to prosecution. Its use of military commissions to accommodate abusive interrogation methods only guarantees more protracted legal battles, and ultimately threatens the nation's ability to achieve justice for the victims and families of September 11.

The administration claims that the Central Intelligence Agency (CIA)'s "enhanced" interrogation program is necessary to protect the nation from another terrorist attack and save American lives. From its inception, however, some government officials warned that the CIA's program was unlawful and inhumane and that it would complicate—and possibly prevent—future prosecutions. These objections were ignored, in part based on the view that such constraints were irrelevant once the goal of law enforcement had shifted from prosecution to prevention.

Several years after coercive interrogation methods were first authorized, the administration was faced with the exact dilemma it had been warned about: what to do about evidence obtained through official cruelty. Rather than repudiate the CIA's methods, or even accept the inadmissibility of the statements obtained, the administration dug itself in deeper, seeking to use military commissions to legitimize the CIA's program. In 2004, the Defense Department established Combatant Status Review Tribunals (CSRTs) and allowed the tribunals to consider statements extracted under torture or through cruel, inhuman or degrading treatment (CID) in deciding whether to detain prisoners as "enemy combatants." In 2006, the administration successfully pressed Congress to include provisions in the Military Commissions Act (MCA) that authorize, for the first time in American history, the admission of coerced confessions as evidence during military commission trials.

In so doing, Congress created a secondary system of defective justice—one that ignores deeply-held American principles of due process and jeopardizes the successful prosecution of terrorist suspects.

This report demonstrates that the use of evidence tainted by torture and other inhuman treatment is pervasive and systematic in the cases of prisoners held at Guantánamo Bay, and has already infected legal judgments made there. It demonstrates that reliance on coerced testimony:

- Threatens the prosecution of those allegedly responsible for the September 11 attacks;

- Taints the legitimacy of the proceedings both at home and in the eyes of the international community, alienating U.S. allies and empowering terrorists;

- Shifts the focus of the proceedings from the suspected criminal conduct of the accused to the abusive conduct of their interrogators;

- Fosters the perception that the cases against suspected terrorists are weak; and

- Validates and perpetuates the use of torture and coercive interrogation techniques.

The report includes case studies of six Guantánamo detainees: Khalid Sheikh Mohammed, Mohammed al-Qahtani, Abu Zubaydah, Mouhamedou Ould Slahi, Binyam Mohamed, and Omar Khadr. All six men allege abuse at the hands of U.S. government interrogators, some of which has been documented by military investigations and detainee interrogation logs, and some of which has been publicly acknowledged by administration officials. Three of these men are among the thirteen who have now been charged with criminal offenses by military commission officials.

Human Rights First has identified at least 62 other suspects currently detained at Guantánamo who also may have been abused. The actual number may be higher. It is impossible to offer an exact calculation because a large portion of the evidence introduced during detention hearings remains classified.

The report includes interviews with experts who have reviewed the latest scientific studies on coercion, and with law enforcement personnel skilled at evaluating the usefulness of coercive tactics for human intelligence gathering and prosecution. The scientific literature belies the assumption that coercion leads to reliable information. Suspects who are tortured or otherwise coerced often provide false or misleading information in order to stop the abuse or because their mental and physical functions have been impaired.

The report also reviews domestic and international laws regarding involuntary statements. Throughout our nation's history, we have abided by an unequivocal prohibition on the use of coerced confessions during criminal trials because, in the words of Chief Justice John Roberts, "we disapprove of such coercion and because such confessions tend to be unreliable."[2] International law also prohibits the use of coerced testimony because the prohibition itself is thought to deter abusive conduct.

Finally, the report discusses the consequences of relying on coerced evidence from the perspectives of legal and military experts, including a source inside the Office of Military Commissions.

Recommendations

Human Rights First recommends:

Criminal Trials

- The U.S. government should try terrorist suspects by court-martial or in civilian criminal courts where coerced confessions are inadmissible, the introduction of hearsay evidence is restricted to protect reliability, and the rules governing the disclosure and introduction of classified evidence are clear.

- In the alternative, Congress should amend the Military Commissions Act to:

  - Prohibit during criminal trials the introduction of evidence obtained through coercion or cruel, inhuman or degrading treatment;

  - Prohibit convictions based on confessions alone and require corroborating evidence of every offense charged;

  - Impose additional discovery requirements on government prosecutors, subject to the same procedures employed in U.S. courts for evaluating potentially classified evidence. These additional requirements should include disclosure of the classified sources, methods and activities by which statements were obtained; and

  - Require the government to prove the reliability and materiality of hearsay evidence it seeks to introduce.

Detention Hearings

- The U.S. government should prohibit the admission of statements extracted through torture or coercion during detention hearings for terrorist suspects. If Combatant Status Review Tribunals are upheld as constitutional, CSRT procedures should be amended to that effect.

- Congress should require the U.S. government to provide detainees with counsel at detention hearings.

- Congress should restore habeas corpus rights to detainees designated as "enemy combatants."

Investigation and Interrogation

- The U.S. government should require government intelligence agents to adhere to the standards of interrogation outlined in the U.S. Army Field Manual.

- Congress should require the videotaping of interrogations of terrorist suspects that occur away from the battlefield.

The Policies and Practices

"The chief mission of U.S. law enforcement...is to stop another attack and apprehend any accomplices to terrorists before they hit us again. If we can't bring them to trial, so be it."
   – Attorney General John Ashcroft, National Security Council Meeting, September 12, 2001
   (as reported by Bob Woodward in *Bush at War*)

"I know that some people question if America is really in a war at all. They view terrorism more as a crime, a problem to be solved mainly with law enforcement and indictments... After the chaos and carnage of September the 11th, it is not enough to serve our enemies with legal papers. The terrorists and their supporters declared war on the United States, and war is what they got."
   – President George W. Bush, State of the Union Address, January 20, 2004

Since the September 11 attacks, the Bush Administration has aggressively promoted "law-free zones," denying the applicability of certain core protections under U.S. and international law to detainees held in secret CIA custody and at Guantánamo Bay. Among these core protections is the right to humane treatment during interrogation. This chapter describes the administration's policies and practices of coercive interrogation and the legal regime created to accommodate them.

The CIA's Coercive Interrogation Techniques

In early 2002, CIA officials reportedly believed that captured al Qaeda suspects were withholding valuable intelligence.[3] They were particularly concerned about a suspect named Abu Zubaydah. It has been widely reported that the Federal Bureau of Investigation (FBI) had already obtained Zubaydah's cooperation using traditional law enforcement methods.[4] Nevertheless,

senior CIA officials are said to have thought that more aggressive interrogation tactics would yield more information more quickly.[5]

The precise moment when CIA interrogators began using abusive interrogation techniques is not known. But in mid-2002, in response to queries about the outer boundaries of permissibility—and likely also to protect interrogators who had already engaged in torture—then-White House Counsel Alberto Gonzales asked the Department of Justice's Office of Legal Counsel (OLC) to interpret interrogation standards under the U.N. Convention Against Torture (CAT). The CAT was ratified by the United States in 1994 and implemented by federal statute, known as the Anti-Torture Act, the same year.[6]

Then-Assistant Attorney General Jay S. Bybee authored one of the OLC opinions. The "Bybee memorandum," as it became known, stated that painful interrogation techniques were permissible so long as the pain caused was less intense than that accompanying organ failure or death. Moreover, if the interrogator's objective was to obtain information—rather than inflict pain—no legal liability would attach, even if severe pain and suffering were "reasonably likely to result."[7] The Bush Administration further took the view that the CAT's prohibition against cruel, inhuman and degrading treatment did not apply to non-citizens held abroad.[8]

Interrogation techniques authorized by the Department of Justice (DoJ) and used by the CIA reportedly included:

- grabbing and shaking prisoners;

- slapping prisoners to cause pain and fear;

- forcing prisoners to stand for upwards of 40 hours;

- exposing prisoners to extremely cold temperatures for prolonged periods and dousing them in cold water;

- waterboarding prisoners by binding them to a board, wrapping their faces in plastic and pouring water over them; or strapping them down, putting a washcloth over their faces and pouring water into their noses;

- confining prisoners in coffin-style boxes;

- keeping prisoners in darkness without access to light; and

- blaring continuous loud music at prisoners. [9] (For a detailed description of the CIA's interrogation techniques, see Appendix C).

The Bybee memorandum was leaked in 2004, causing enormous public outcry. Thereafter, the Justice Department repudiated the memo, and CIA Inspector General John Helgerson found that the agency's interrogation techniques constituted cruel, inhuman and degrading treatment.[10] In December 2004, the Bybee memorandum was officially replaced by another memorandum that included a new analysis of the torture prohibition. But the new memorandum does not disavow the President's commander-in-chief authority to authorize torture, nor does it explicitly define torture or even state that any specific interrogation techniques are prohibited.[11]

In response to the disclosures about abuse at Abu Ghraib and leaks of the Bybee memorandum and other administration documents justifying abuse, in 2005, Congress passed the Detainee Treatment Act (DTA), which prohibits the use of cruel, inhuman or degrading treatment of prisoners in U.S. government custody.[12] In 2006, the Supreme Court held in *Hamdan v. Rumsfeld* that the humane treatment requirements of Common Article 3 of the Geneva Conventions apply to captured al Qaeda suspects.[13]

After *Hamdan*, the CIA temporarily suspended its "enhanced interrogation program."[14] But it appears to be up and running again. On July 20, 2007, the president issued Executive Order No. 13440 purporting to interpret Common Article 3 as applied to interrogation. The order not only fails to rule out the use of "enhanced" techniques, but it actually appears to permit "willful and outrageous acts of personal abuse" so long as their purpose is to gain intelligence rather than to humiliate or degrade the prisoner.[15] During a television interview in October 2007, CIA Director General Michael Hayden acknowledged the agency's continued use of harsh techniques. Although he declined to discuss specific practices, he stated that they may include methods that are prohibited in military interrogations.[16] In addition, although Attorney General Michael Mukasey has said that waterboarding is not part of the CIA's current program, he has refused to say whether it is illegal under all circumstances, or to rule it out as a future interrogation technique.[17]

The Military's Coercive Interrogation Techniques

In October 2002, under pressure to obtain intelligence, Joint Task Force 170 (JTF-170), the military interrogation unit stationed at Guantánamo, sought to use "more aggressive interrogation techniques" on detainees.[18] The request came just two months after the Bybee memorandum was written, opening the door for approval of abusive tactics. On December 2, 2002, then-Secretary of Defense Donald Rumsfeld approved various harsh techniques, including:

- "interrogator identity" (interrogator impersonates a citizen or interrogator from a country known for harsh treatment of prisoners);

- stress positions, such as standing, for up to four hours;

- isolation for up to 30 days, with extensions beyond 30 days upon Commanding General approval;

- deprivation of all light and auditory stimuli;

- hooding during transportation and questioning;

- 20-hour interrogations;

- the use of a prisoner's individual phobias, such as fear of dogs, to induce stress; and

- light pushing.[19]

Numerous military personnel and lawyers objected to the use of these techniques, including the Commander of the Criminal Investigation Task Force, Colonel Brittain P. Mallow, and Navy General Counsel Alberto Mora. Mora described the techniques as "at a minimum, cruel and unusual treatment and, at worst, torture."[20] In response to the criticism, in January 2003, Secretary Rumsfeld rescinded his approval of the techniques and authorized a working group to make further recommendations.[21] In April 2003, Secretary Rumsfeld personally approved a new list, which included:

- dietary manipulation;

- hooding and other sensory deprivation techniques;

- environmental manipulation;

- sleep adjustment;

- "false flag" (leading prisoners to believe that they have been transferred to a country that permits torture); and

- isolation.[22]

These techniques appear to have been part of Guantánamo interrogation policy until March 2005, when the Pentagon declared the Working Group report a "non-operational 'historical' document."[23]

Coerced Evidence at Guantánamo

CSRTs Rely on Coerced Evidence to Support Detention

The Defense Department (DoD) established Combatant Status Review Tribunals (CSRTs) in response to two 2004 Supreme Court rulings holding that Guantánamo detainees must be permitted to challenge their detention before neutral decision makers.[24] The order establishing CSRTs expressly states that detainees have already been judged enemy combatants "through multiple levels of review by officers of the Department of Defense" before their hearings.[25] Thus, three-member panels of military officers simply review prior enemy combatant determinations made by their superiors. Administrative Review Boards (ARBs) subsequently conduct annual status reviews.

CSRT panels may consider any information "relevant and helpful to a resolution of the issues," and they must presume that the evidence presented is "genuine and accurate."[26] There is no prohibition against evidence obtained through coercion or even torture. The DTA provides only that CSRTs consider "(A) whether any statement derived from or relating to such detainee was obtained as a result of coercion; and (B) the probative value (if any) of any such statement."[27]

From 2004 to 2007, more than 570 CSRT hearings were conducted, with all but 38 detainees designated as enemy combatants.[28] The detainees had no meaningful opportunity to contest their designations, no legal representation at their hearings, and no access to classified evidence.[29] Even CSRT panel members were denied access to relevant classified evidence and were presented primarily with post-detention custodial and interrogation reports regarding other detainees. In addition, administration-imposed time limitations and budget constraints precluded CSRT panels from hearing from witnesses from outside Guantánamo.[30] Due at least in part to these limitations, CSRT panel members made little effort to assess the veracity of detainees' allegations

---

Definitions

Torture: An act specifically intended to inflict severe physical or mental pain or suffering (other than pain or suffering incidental to lawful sanctions) upon another person in custody or under physical control. "Severe mental pain or suffering" is defined as the prolonged mental harm caused by or resulting from (A) the intentional infliction or threatened infliction of severe physical pain or suffering; (B) the administration or application, or threatened administration or application, of mind-altering substances or other procedures calculated to disrupt profoundly the senses or the personality; (C) the threat of imminent death; or (D) the threat that another person will imminently be subjected to death, severe physical pain or suffering, or the administration or application of mind-altering substances or other procedures calculated to disrupt profoundly the senses or personality.[31]

Cruel, Inhuman or Degrading Treatment: The cruel, unusual, and inhuman treatment prohibited by the Fifth, Eighth, and Fourteenth Amendments to the Constitution of the United States. The Supreme Court has long considered prisoner treatment to violate the Fifth and Fourteenth Amendments if the treatment "shocks the conscience."[32] The Eighth Amendment standards have been incorporated into the Fifth and Fourteenth Amendment due process analysis by the Court, which determined that individuals detained by the state who have not been convicted by a court enjoy at least the same level of rights as convicted criminals.[33]

The Bush Administration interprets the "shocks the conscience" test as requiring an evaluation of conduct on a sliding scale, allowing for increasingly aggressive interrogation techniques as the government's interest in a particular interrogation increases.[34] Thus, it explicitly leaves open the possibility of using cruel interrogation techniques on a detainee believed to have crucial intelligence information. This interpretation blurs the line of prohibited conduct to the point where any cruel treatment may be justified if needed for intelligence purposes.

---

of innocence or abuse. In fact, in a number of instances, panel members failed even to wait for the results of abuse investigations before making their determinations.[35]

Finally, detainees were not entitled to meaningful review of their designations. The writ of habeas corpus traditionally allows for a speedy opportunity to contest the factual basis for detention, with the assistance of counsel, before a neutral decision maker. The DTA, however, only permits detainees to file challenges to the D.C. Circuit Court of Appeals, and it does not allow them to rebut the government's evidence or the means by which it was obtained—only to address whether the government adhered to its own procedures and whether the procedures were lawful.[36] In fact, the D.C. Circuit must presume the accuracy of evidence presented to CSRT panels, even where it was withheld as classified from detainees. At issue in the consolidated cases of *Boumediene v. Bush* and *Al-Odah v. United States*, now under consideration by the Supreme Court, is whether this limited DTA review provides an adequate substitute for traditional habeas review.[37]

The MCA Allows Coerced Evidence at Trial

The Bush Administration has consistently maintained that detainees who are designated enemy combatants are not protected by the U.S. Constitution and are outside the jurisdiction of federal courts.[38] Prior to 2004, the administration also contended that the CAT did not apply to non-citizens held outside the United States.[39] The administration further argued that detainees were not entitled to the protections of the Third Geneva Convention Relative to the Treatment of Prisoners of War, or to the determination of prisoner of war (POW) status, or even to the minimum humane treatment standards of Common Article 3. The administration position thus allowed unchecked executive branch discretion in the treatment and prosecution of detainees at secret detention facilities and at Guantánamo (and set the stage for the migration of abusive interrogation practices to Afghanistan and Iraq).

The Supreme Court, however, struck down several key components of the administration's legal theories in three critical opinions in 2004 and 2006.[40] The last decision from that period was *Hamdan v. Rumsfeld*, which rejected the military commissions as originally created by President Bush. The *Hamdan* Court held that the commissions violated the Uniform Code of Military Justice and the Geneva Conventions.[41]

Following the Supreme Court's decision in *Hamdan*, the Bush Administration obtained congressional authorization through the Military Commissions Act of 2006 (MCA) for a military commission regime that would allow it to perpetuate and exploit many of its previous legal theories. The MCA expressly authorizes the admission of statements obtained by coercion, provided that "the totality of the circumstances renders the statement[s] reliable and possessing sufficient probative value" and their introduction serves the "best interest of justice." It even permits the introduction of statements obtained by cruel, inhuman or degrading treatment (CID), provided the statements satisfy the above requirements and were obtained prior to the enactment of the DTA.[42]

The MCA ostensibly excludes evidence "obtained by use of torture."[43] But it does not specify which interrogation methods constitute torture, thus leaving it up to military commission judges to draw the line between torture and CID. (See textbox above). Testifying before the Senate Judiciary Committee in December 2007, Brigadier General Thomas W. Hartmann, legal advisor to the DoD's appointing authority for military commissions, declined to say whether statements extracted through waterboarding would be barred as torture evidence. Rather he explained, "[i]f the evidence is reliable and probative, and the judge concludes that it is in the best interest of justice to introduce that evidence...those are the rules we will follow. Those are the rules we must follow."[44]

As far as the Bush Administration is concerned, none of the CIA's interrogation techniques—including waterboarding—constitutes torture under the circumstances in which they have been used. Attorney General Michael Mukasey has said that waterboarding may be illegal under certain circumstances but permissible under others. He describes

the matter as a "balancing test of the value of doing something as against the cost of doing it."[45] Taking the analysis a step further, Assistant Attorney General Steven Bradbury has specifically approved the CIA's use of waterboarding, stating: "Our office has advised the CIA when they were proposing to use waterboarding that the use of the procedure subject to strict limitations and safeguards applicable to the program was not torture—did not violate the anti-torture statute, and I think that conclusion was reasonable."[46]

Other MCA Rules Compound Effects of Coerced Evidence Provisions

At a press conference in February 2008, Brig. Gen. Hartmann claimed the "processes that we have before the military commissions in many ways parallel the military justice system," and "[w]e are going to give [the detainees] rights that are virtually identical to the rights we provide our military members."[47] This is simply not the case. Not only are the lines between torture and CID blurred under the MCA, but three additional provisions in the MCA deprive suspects of basic rights present in the civilian and military justice systems. These provisions render the threshold test of reliability almost meaningless.

First, in a departure from long-standing principles of due process, the MCA expressly permits the admission of second-hand or hearsay evidence, and places the burden on the defendant to prove that evidence is unreliable or lacking in probative value.[48] This Catch-22 makes it impossible for the defendant to confront and cross-examine the original source of the evidence, which is often the only effective way to demonstrate unreliability.

Second, under certain circumstances, the MCA permits the government to withhold from discovery the classified sources, methods and activities by which evidence was obtained.[49]

Third, no corroboration is required for admission of coerced statements under the military commission rules.[50] Whether or not a military commission may convict based on uncorroborated statements alone remains an open question. Corroboration of even non-coerced confessions is required during courts-martial and in civilian courts.[51]

Ultimately, a number of scenarios could lead to convictions—and even executions—based on coerced evidence.

First, a military judge could permit the introduction of a detainee's coerced statements without requiring corroborating evidence or disclosure of the specific interrogation methods used on the detainee. The prosecutor could assert that the interrogation methods are classified and refuse to provide access to the interrogators or to interrogation transcripts or notes.

Second, the prosecution could introduce incriminating hearsay statements (or summaries of those statements) that, unbeknownst to the defendant or his counsel, were obtained from a third-party witness through coercion. The prosecution could assert that the witness's identity and the interrogation methods used on the witness are classified and refuse to provide interrogation transcripts or notes, or access to the witnesses for examination. In some cases, it may be relatively simple to ascertain the sources of the information because the treatment of some detainees has been revealed publicly by government sources. But, in other instances, defendants could be denied access to less notorious witnesses, whom the government keeps behind a curtain of classification, making it impossible for detainees to establish that information was obtained through coercion, let alone that the information is unreliable. Even military judges might be denied access to information necessary to determine whether particular statements were coerced, and to assess their reliability.

Third, the prosecution could withhold important exculpatory evidence from the accused by asserting that the evidence is classified, thus denying the defendant an adequate opportunity to mount a proper defense.

The Case Studies

"Have any of these guys ever tried to talk to someone who's been deprived of his clothes? ...He's going to be ashamed, and he's going to be humiliated, and cold. He'll tell you anything you want to hear to get his clothes back. There's no value in it."

– Former FBI Agent Dan Coleman (as reported by Jane Mayer in "Outsourcing Torture," *New Yorker*, February 14, 2005)

Nearly 800 men have been imprisoned at Guantánamo since 2002.[52] The vast majority have been released without charge. Approximately 280 detainees remain, roughly 80 of whom the government says it intends to charge.[53]

At this writing, however, only one man has been convicted, and charges have been sworn against just fourteen others. Australian David Hicks was sentenced to nine months in prison following a guilty plea in March 2007. Omar Khadr and Salim Ahmed Hamdan are engaged in pretrial proceedings, and their trials are expected to begin in 2008. Charges against four others, Mohammed Jawad, Ahmed Mohammed Ahmed al Darbi, Ibrahim Mahmoud al Qosi, and Ali Hamza Ahmed Sulayman al Bahlul have been referred. Charges against Mohammed Kamin and Ahmed Khalfan Ghailani were sworn in March 2008. The six remaining men, Khalid Sheikh Mohammed, Mohammed al-Qahtani, Walid Muahmmed Salih Mubarek bin Attash, Ramzi Binalshibh,

Ali Abdul Aziz Ali, and Mustafa Ahmed Adam al-Hawsawi have been jointly charged with participating in the planning and execution of the September 11 attacks.[54]

Human Rights First has identified at least 68 detainees who allege abuse in custody. (See Appendix B). Our findings are based primarily on CSRT and ARB transcripts, news accounts from credible media sources, interviews with attorneys representing detainees, and the Detainee Abuse and Accountability Project, undertaken jointly by Human Rights First, the Center for Human Rights and Global Justice at NYU School of Law, and Human Rights Watch.[55]

The following case studies focus on six men, three of whom have already been charged. Some of the abuses described have been documented in military investigations and prisoner interrogation logs, and some have been publicly acknowledged by administration officials.

Khalid Sheikh Mohammed

Khalid Sheikh Mohammed

Khalid Sheikh Moham-med, the reputed al Qaeda mastermind of some 31 terrorist plots, was apprehended in Pakistan in March 2003 and transferred to Guantánamo from secret CIA custody in September 2006.[56] At Guantánamo, he was deemed a "high-value" detainee and held without charge for 16 months. In February 2008, prosecutors referred charges against Mohammed and five other Guantánamo detainees allegedly linked to the September 11 attacks. The charges, for which prosecutors are seeking the death penalty, include conspiracy, murder, attacking civilians, terrorism, and providing material support for terrorism. Mohammed is accused of proposing the September 11 attacks to Osama bin Laden, obtaining bin Laden's funding and approval for the attacks, training the hijackers, and generally overseeing the operation.[57]

Mohammed's trial is expected to be the centerpiece of the military commission proceedings at Guantánamo Bay. Why, then, has there been so much delay? The initial delay can be attributed to the Bush Administration itself, which concealed Mohammed in CIA custody for three-and-a-half years rather than produce him for prosecution. CIA Director Michael Hayden has acknowledged that CIA interrogators waterboarded Mohammed.[58] As a "high-value" detainee, Mohammed also was subjected to other "enhanced" techniques, the details of which have been withheld as classified from public view. Reportedly, however, interrogators placed Mohammed in positions of stress and duress, induced hypothermia, subjected him to prolonged sleep deprivation, threatened to harm his children, and engaged in other unspecified techniques up to 100 times over a two-week period.[59]

Although government officials insist that Mohammed disclosed critical intelligence,[60] it has also been reported that he wove in numerous falsehoods, making it difficult for interrogators to distinguish fiction from fact.[61] Some interrogators have suggested that the use of torture and cruel treatment undermined their ability to develop a rapport with Mohammed and in fact destroyed his credibility.[62] One CIA official reportedly characterized many of Mohammed's claims as "'white noise'–designed to send the U.S. on wild goose chases or to get him through the day's interrogation session."[63]

Within three weeks of his capture, reports suggested that Mohammed had provided the names and descriptions of about twelve al Qaeda members planning terrorist attacks.[64] However, official statements regarding Mohammed's interrogations sent to Washington reportedly began with the caveat: "the detainee has been known to withhold information or deliberately mislead."[65] One former CIA analyst has said: "It's difficult to give credence to any particular area of this large a charge sheet that he confessed to, considering the situation he found himself in. K.S.M. [Khalid Sheikh Mohammed] has no prospect of ever seeing freedom again, so his only gratification in life is to portray himself as the James Bond of jihadism."[66]

The Bush Administration was responsible for yet more delay after Mohammed's delivery to Guantánamo: the CIA's use of torture, and Mohammed's own questionable credibility left prosecutors needing time to shore up their case. FBI and military interrogators known as the "Clean Team" are said to have spent months at Guantánamo questioning Mohammed, his co-defendants, and potential witnesses again, this time with non-confrontational, rapport-building techniques. The charges that followed are supposedly based in part on information provided during that time.[67]

But swearing charges is just the initial step in any prosecution, and a trial is still a long way off. Additional delays undoubtedly will follow as the parties argue over the reliability of the suspects' more recent statements, and the military commission judge is charged with

Did Khalid Sheikh Mohammed Lie under Torture about Other Detainees?

Ali Saleh Khallah al-Marri: Al-Marri has been in military custody in a naval brig in Charleston, South Carolina for four-and-a-half years, since being designated an enemy combatant by President Bush in June 2003. He was held incommunicado and denied access to counsel for 16 months.[68] During that time, he was allegedly denied basic necessities and was interrogated under abusive conditions. The public explanation for al-Marri's ongoing detention is a Department of Defense (DoD) statement that he plotted with Khalid Sheikh Mohammed as part of a "sleeper cell" to commit terrorist attacks in the United States. [69] DoD likely relied on statements made by Khalid Sheikh Mohammed under interrogation in constructing these allegations. Some, if not all, of Mohammed's statements were probably obtained through torture and cruel treatment. Yet al-Marri has not had the opportunity to rebut Mohammed's allegations because his lawyers have been denied access to Mohammed.

A three-judge panel of the United States Court of Appeals for the Fourth Circuit ruled in June 2007 that al-Marri's indefinite detention in military custody was unconstitutional and warned that avoiding criminal prosecution "in order to interrogate him without the strictures of criminal process" would be illegal.[70] The U.S. government obtained an *en banc* rehearing, which automatically vacated that decision. The *en banc* hearing was held on October 31, 2007, but the fourth circuit has not yet issued its decision.

Riduan Isamuddin (also known as Hambali): Hambali is being held as a "high-value" detainee at Guantánamo, but no formal charges have been filed against him. He was captured in late 2003 and deemed an enemy combatant following a CSRT hearing on April 4, 2007. If Hambali is eventually charged, statements made by Khalid Sheikh Mohammed during abusive interrogations may be introduced against him at his trial. Most likely, Mohammed's statements already were introduced against Hambali during the classified portion of his CSRT hearing. In September 2006, President Bush announced that Mohammed had identified Hambali as a "suspected terrorist leader" and "the leader of al Qaeda's Southeast Asian affiliate known as 'J-I [Jemiah Islamia].'" President Bush further stated that Mohammed had identified Hambali's brother as "the leader of a 'J-I' cell and Hambali's conduit for communications with al Qaeda."[71]

Majid Khan: Majid Khan, a U.S. resident, was held in secret CIA custody for more than three years before being transferred to Guantánamo Bay as a "high-value" detainee in September 2006. If Khan is eventually charged by military commission, statements made by Khalid Sheikh Mohammed during abusive interrogations could be introduced against him. Most likely, statements made by Mohammed already were introduced against Khan during the classified portion of his CSRT hearing. In September 2006, President Bush stated that Mohammed had revealed during interrogation that Khan "had been told to deliver $50,000 to individuals working for...Hambali." President Bush further stated that Khan had confirmed Mohammed's version of events when confronted with the information.[72] However, the reliability of Khan's confession is also in doubt: Khan's lawyers claim he was repeatedly tortured by CIA interrogators and was "submitted to [redacted] interrogation tactics that have long been prohibited by U.S. civil and military law."[73] His lawyers recently filed a motion requesting an order declaring that the interrogation methods used on Khan constituted torture and other forms of impermissible coercion.[74]

Mod Farik bin Amin (also known as Zubair): Zubair is being held as a "high-value" detainee at Guantánamo Bay. He was deemed an enemy combatant following a CSRT hearing on March 13, 2007. If he is eventually charged by military commission, Khalid Sheikh Mohammed's statements made during abusive interrogations could be introduced against him and were likely already introduced against him during his CSRT hearing. It has been reported that Mohammed stated under interrogation that Majid Khan delivered money to Zubair and also provided Zubair's phone number.[75]

determining whether the FBI's rapport-building methods can overcome the taint of the CIA's harsh interrogation techniques. Would Mohammed and the others have responded to FBI interrogators without having been tortured beforehand by the CIA? If the military commission judge answers "no," then she will have to decide whether waterboarding constitutes torture under the MCA, or whether it falls into the category of mere coercion or CID. Further complications will ensue if the CIA continues to shield as classified the other interrogation methods it used on Mohammed or the identity of the interrogators, a position which is entirely permissible under the MCA.[76]

Did Al-Qahtani Lie under Torture about Other Detainees?

Marc Falkoff, a lawyer who represents three Guantánamo detainees, alleges that al-Qahtani lied about his clients under torture and that al-Qahtani's false statements have served as the basis for his clients' detention.

Abd Al Malik: Abd Al Malik was captured in Afghanistan in late 2002, and he is being held as an enemy combatant at Guantánamo. In 2005, Falkoff wrote a letter to the ARB, contesting Al Malik's enemy combatant designation and present dangerousness. In the letter, Falkoff alleges that Al Malik's CSRT hearing was fundamentally unfair on two grounds. First, according to Falkoff, the CSRT panel considered Al Malik's own statements made after he had been deprived of sleep and threatened with torture, rape and violence against his family. Second, the panel considered incriminating statements regarding Al Malik made under torture by Mohammed al-Qahtani.

Falkoff refers to a 2004 letter written by T.J. Harrington, then-deputy assistant director of the Counterterrorism Division of the FBI. In the letter, Harrington voices his concern about abusive interrogation tactics he witnessed at Guantánamo, including those employed on al-Qahtani. The copy of Falkoff's letter sent to Human Rights First has been heavily redacted. But Falkoff's conclusion is clear:

"It should be apparent from this FBI letter that Detainee 063's [Mohammed al-Qahtani's] incriminating statements about Abu Al Malik are patently untrustworthy in light of the abuse he suffered. This detainee had every reason to implicate as an al Qaeda associate anyone that interrogators asked him to implicate since the punishment for failing to cooperate was extreme isolation—while the reward for cooperation was a promised release from prison."[77]

Faruq Ali Ahmed: Faruq Ali Ahmed was arrested in Afghanistan in 2001 and is being held as an enemy combatant at Guantánamo. In 2005, Falkoff wrote a letter to the ARB on Ahmed's behalf, similar to the one he wrote about Al Malik, and citing the same letter by Deputy Assistant Director Harrington describing al-Qahtani's abuse. Portions of this letter sent to Human Rights First have also been redacted. But Falkoff clearly concludes that Ahmed's enemy combatant designation was unconstitutional, and explains:

"Faruq is not now and never has been associated with al Qaeda. The only evidence of such an association comes from a proven liar and from another detainee who was abused and coerced into making statements inculpating other men."[78]

Uthman Abdul Rahim Mohammed Uthman: Uthman Abdul Rahim Mohammed Uthman is also being held as an enemy combatant at Guantánamo. In a letter to the ARB on Uthman's behalf, also redacted, Falkoff again references al-Qahtani's abuse, and laments that the CSRT panel considering Uthman's designation did not have access to Deputy Assistant Director Harrington's letter.[79]

It remains to be seen how military judges will reach resolution on these issues or whether the military commission system itself will retain any semblance of credibility after the pretrial hearings in Mohammed's case. But if the case does eventually proceed to trial, the gravity of Mohammed's alleged offenses may be overshadowed by legal battles over classified evidence, waterboarding, and the other harsh interrogation techniques he endured.

In the meantime, the statements Mohammed made under torture already may have been used during CSRTs as a basis for holding other detainees without charge, and could be used again if these detainees are ever tried. Among others, Mohammed is reported to have provided information about at least three other "high-value" detainees awaiting trial at Guantánamo, and about Ali Saleh Khallah al-Marri, the only enemy combatant being held on U.S. soil. (See textbox above). The MCA's rules on hearsay and classification allow the introduction of Mohammed's statements at these detainees' trials without calling Mohammed as a witness or even necessarily identifying him by name as the source of information.

Mohammed al-Qahtani

Mohammed al-Qahtani

Mohammed al-Qahtani, the alleged "20th hijacker" in the September 11 attacks, was sent to Guantánamo in February 2002, where he was held without charge for six years.[80] In February 2008, al-Qahtani was charged as one of six co-conspirators with participating in the planning and execution of the September 11 attacks.[81] Al-Qahtani is the only one of the six who was not held in secret CIA custody and who is not classified as a "high-value" detainee.

Guantánamo officials reportedly did not discover al-Qahtani's true identity until July 2002, upon which he was marked for intensive interrogation.[82] According to the Department of Defense, during the summer and fall of 2002, al-Qahtani resisted standard interrogation techniques, prompting military officials to question whether "there may be more flexibility in the type of techniques we use on him."[83] On October 11, 2002, Major General Michael E. Dunlavey, Commander of Joint Task Force 170, sought approval from the chain-of-command for an interrogation plan, known as the "First Special Interrogation Plan," that included 19 techniques outside the U.S. Army Field Manual. Military interrogators began using these techniques on al-Qahtani soon after they received preliminary approval.[84] Some details of the interrogation regime were revealed in 2005 with the release of an executive summary to a report regarding allegations of abuse at Guantánamo. Further details were disclosed when al-Qahtani's military interrogation log was leaked from Guantánamo.[85]

By the fall of 2002, al-Qahtani had been "subjected to intense isolation for over three months" and "was evidencing behavior consistent with extreme psychological trauma (talking to non-existent people, reporting hearing voices, crouching in a cell covered with a sheet for hours on end)."[86] He was interrogated for 18 to 20 hours each day for 48 of the next 54 days and was subjected to at least ten additional techniques, including sleep deprivation, forced standing and other stress positions, and sexual and other physical humiliation.[87] The latter included strip-searches, forced nudity in front of a female interrogator, placing pictures of women in swimsuits around his neck and a thong on his head, and forcing him to wear a bra. By October 2002, a dog had been used to intimidate him.[88] In addition, al-Qahtani was allegedly led around by a leash tied to his chains and told to bark like a dog and growl at pictures of terrorists.[89] In order to keep his body functioning during physically coercive interrogations, officials reportedly gave him enemas and administered intravenous fluids and drugs. At one point, al-Qahtani's heart rate fell to 35 beats per minute, but he was subjected to more questioning less than 48 hours after being revived.[90]

The Defense Department maintains that al-Qahtani disclosed valuable intelligence about recruitment, logistics and planning for the September 11 attacks. Specifically, the agency asserts that al-Qahtani provided information about 30 of Osama bin Laden's bodyguards, clarified Jose Padilla's and Richard Reid's relationship with al Qaeda and their activities in Afghanistan, and provided additional information about Adnan El Shukrijumah, a suspected al Qaeda operative.[91] In March 2006, however, al-Qahtani repudiated all of his previous statements through a lawyer, claiming they were extracted as a result of torture.[92] During his ARB hearing in October 2006, al-Qahtani again said he had repeatedly lied under interrogation and had "adopt[ed] the story that the interrogators wanted to hear." He further stated: "Once this torture stopped, I explained over and over that none of what I said was true."[93]

Before the government swore charges against al-Qahtani in February 2008, many people—including key Guantánamo insiders—believed his prosecution would be impossible because of the abuse he endured. This list of people included Colonel Brittain P. Mallow, former commander of the Criminal Investigative Task Force (CITF), and Mark Fallow, CITF's former deputy commander.[94] Whether or not al-Qahtani's trial eventually proceeds, the six-year delay can be attributed largely to the use of coercive methods approved by the Bush Administration in his case. Former Secretary of Defense Rumsfeld himself specifically authorized those techniques.[95]

It remains to be seen whether the government's case against al-Qahtani has changed in any significant respect in recent months. Al-Qahtani has civilian counsel, so he may not have been re-interrogated by the "Clean Team." Nonetheless, his case may turn in part on new statements elicited by this team from other detainees.

In the alternative, if the government has not collected additional evidence from al-Qahtani or other detainees, prosecutors may attempt to rely on statements he made under abuse. The MCA provides some cover for interrogators' coercive tactics. If the military commission judge decides that al-Qahtani was subjected to coercion or CID, but not torture, his statements might be admissible against him. Nonetheless, while the MCA may shortcut the admissibility problem, it does not legitimize the abusive interrogation methods. In fact, the MCA's provisions on coerced evidence only increase the risk that al-Qahtani's trial and appeal will be dominated by debate over the abusive conduct of his interrogators, rather than his alleged criminal acts.

Whether or not al-Qahtani is eventually tried, the statements he made under torture may well have been introduced during the CSRT hearings of at least three other detainees, each of whom continues to be held without charge at Guantánamo. Additional statements made by al-Qahtani also may have been introduced during the CSRTs of Osama bin Laden's alleged bodyguards and could be introduced against some or all of these detainees during their military commission trials. (See textbox on p.14). The MCA's rules on hearsay and classification allow the introduction of al-Qahtani's statements without requiring him to testify, or even necessarily requiring the prosecutor to identify him by name as the source of information, thus potentially

allowing prosecutors to conceal that the statements were elicited under coercion.

Abu Zubaydah

Abu Zubaydah

Abu Zubaydah is an alleged al Qaeda leader and close associate of Osama bin Laden. He was apprehended in 2002 following a firefight in Pakistan, during the course of which he was shot three times, suffering serious injuries. After receiving medical attention at a hospital in Lahore, Zubaydah was transported to a secret detention facility in Thailand where he was interrogated.[96]

Initially, FBI agents questioned Zubaydah employing standard methods.[97] Official government sources have said they obtained useful intelligence on al Qaeda using these techniques. Reportedly, Zubaydah confirmed Khalid Sheikh Mohammed's role in the September 11 attacks and provided information leading to Jose Padilla's arrest in May 2002.[98] At the same time, however, CIA officials reportedly believed that more information could be elicited from Zubaydah more quickly using "aggressive" techniques.[99] Thus, the CIA sought and received authorization to use some alternative methods. In the words of President Bush:

> We knew that Zubaydah had more information that could save innocent lives, but he stopped talking. As his questioning proceeded, it became clear that he had received training on how to resist interrogation. And so the CIA used an alternative set of procedures... .I cannot describe the specific methods used... .But I can say the procedures were tough, and they were safe, and lawful, and necessary.[100]

Videotaping Interrogations

The CIA has admitted to videotaping the interrogations of Abu Zubaydah and a second alleged al Qaeda leader named Abd al Rahim al Nashiri. But those videotapes were ultimately destroyed. Whether additional terrorist suspects also were videotaped by the CIA remains unclear.

Many experts and some members of Congress believe that videotaping should be required. Representative Rush Holt (D-NJ), for example, put forward legislation in the 108th Congress to mandate the videotaping of all future detainee interrogations.[101] Experts point out that videotaping would not only protect suspects from illegal abuse; it would also protect interviewers who act lawfully by providing evidence to rebut erroneous claims of abuse by prisoners. Furthermore, videotaping would assist in analyzing specific interrogations. The Army Field Manual even states a preference for videotaping interrogations: "[V]ideo recording is possibly the most accurate method of recording a questioning session since it records not only the voices but also can be examined for details of body language and source and collector interaction."[102] Finally, videotaping would enable the study of and improvement upon interrogation methods as a whole. The United States has not, in any scientific manner, studied the effectiveness of its interrogation methods since WW II.

In February 2008, CIA Director Michael Hayden publicly acknowledged that CIA interrogators waterboarded Zubaydah.[103] Based on one press account, which cites current and former intelligence and law enforcement officials, Zubaydah also was stripped naked, exposing his injuries, subjected to so much air-conditioning that he "seemed to turn blue," and blasted with rock music.[104] Additionally, according to CIA sources, Zubaydah "was slapped, grabbed, made to stand long hours in a cold cell, and finally handcuffed and strapped feet up to a water board until after 0.31 seconds he begged for mercy and began to cooperate."[105] Another account adds that Zubaydah was threatened with death, denied medication, and subjected to loud and continuous noise and harsh lights.[106] Current and former intelligence officials have said that the CIA suspended the use of harsh techniques on Zubaydah in June or July 2002.[107]

The CIA videotaped at least several hundred hours of Zubaydah's interrogations, but the tapes were destroyed in November 2005 at the behest of Jose Rodriguez, the CIA's former director of clandestine operations.[108] (See textbox above). Rodriguez's decision to destroy the tapes is the subject of ongoing congressional and criminal investigations. Director Hayden has asserted that the tapes were destroyed to protect the identities of the interrogators and because they no longer had intelligence value. Many others, however, believe they were destroyed to shield the interrogators—and senior government

officials who authorized their behavior—from prosecution for criminal conduct captured in the recordings.[109]

Although Zubaydah has been held at Guantánamo since September 2006, military prosecutors have still not filed any charges against him, most likely because the accuracy of his statements—and the legitimacy of the process by which they were extracted—remain in dispute.[110] The CIA insists that Zubaydah provided reliable information regarding members of the al Qaeda leadership, including Khalid Sheikh Mohammed, and reliable threat information that "disrupted a number of attacks..."[111] However, Zubaydah himself claims he lied to satisfy his interrogators. The following exchange occurred during his CSRT hearing:

President:	In your previous statement, you were saying specific treatments. Can you describe a little bit more about what those treatments were?
Detainee:	[REDACTED]
President:	I understand.
Detainee:	And they not give me chance all this [REDACTED]
President:	So I understand that during this treatment, you said things to make them stop and then those statements were actually untrue, is that correct?
Detainee:	Yes.[112]

Dan Coleman, a retired FBI agent who worked on Zubaydah's case, also believes Zubaydah lied. Coleman says the CIA's harsh techniques, together with Zubaydah's own mental problems, cast doubt on Zubaydah's importance to al Qaeda and on his credibility. "I don't have confidence in anything he says, because once you go down that road, everything [he] say[s] is tainted," said Coleman in reference to the coercive techniques. "He was talking before they did that to him, but they didn't believe him. The problem is they didn't realize he didn't know all that much."[113]

That prosecutors still have not charged Zubaydah may indicate that they cannot do so without relying on his statements obtained under abuse. The MCA's provisions on coerced and classified evidence provide prosecutors with one avenue. As long as the military commission judge assigned to Zubaydah's case defines waterboarding as coercion or CID, rather than as torture, his statements might be admissible at trial. In addition, the MCA permits prosecutors to shield as classified the details of other interrogation methods used on Zubaydah. However, while the MCA may cure the admissibility problem, it does not legitimize the CIA's methods in the eyes of the public. Without public trust in the proceedings, the legitimacy of Zubaydah's trial will be in question, and justice will be undermined.

The CIA's cruel treatment of Zubaydah also may infect the trials of other Guantánamo detainees. Reportedly, five detainees were arrested based on information provided by or related to Zubaydah.[114]

Mohamedou Ould Slahi

Mohamedou Ould Slahi

Mohamedou Ould Slahi allegedly steered Ramzi Binalshibh and three of the September 11 terrorist hijackers to Osama bin Laden.[115] He has been detained at Guantánamo for close to five years without charge.

A military investigation into the treatment of detainees at Guantánamo confirmed that, from July to September 2003, interrogators subjected Slahi to environmental manipulation, changing the air conditioner to cause extreme temperatures, threatened to interrogate and detain his mother at Guantánamo, and threatened his family if he failed to cooperate.[116] Slahi also alleges that he was held in isolation, beaten, and sexually humiliated.[117] An intelligence memorandum from August 2003 reports that an interrogator told Slahi:

> [B]eatings and physical pain are not the worst thing in the world. After all, after being beaten for a while, humans tend to disconnect the mind from the body and make it through. However, there are worse things than physical pain. Interrogator assured Detainee that, eventually, he will talk, because everyone does. But until then, he will very soon disappear down a very dark hole. His very existence will become erased. His electronic files will be deleted from the computer, his paper files will be packed up and filed away, and his existence will be forgotten by all. No one will know what happened to him and, eventually, no one will care.[118]

Lieutenant Colonel V. Stuart Couch, the military prosecutor originally assigned to Slahi's case, stated that he first suspected that Slahi had been abused when he was provided with a sudden and unexplained increase in intelligence reports on the case. Before then, Lt. Col. Couch says he had little evidence against Slahi.[119] Lt. Col. Couch then made repeated requests to intelligence

The View from Inside: Military Commission Prosecutors Resign Over Process

"I had instructed the prosecutors in September 2005 that we would not offer any evidence derived by waterboarding, one of the aggressive interrogation techniques the administration has sanctioned. [Defense Department General Counsel William J.] Haynes and I have different perspectives and support different agendas, and the decision to give him command over the chief prosecutor's office, in my view, cast a shadow over the integrity of military commissions."

— Former Chief Prosecutor Colonel Morris Davis, December 29, 2007[120]

Defense lawyers are not alone in voicing concerns about detainee abuse and military commission procedures. Since 2004, at least four military commission prosecutors—including Lt. Col. Couch—have refused to prosecute detainees or have resigned over concerns that the process is politicized.

In March 2004, Former Military Commission Prosecutor Captain John Carr (now a major) and Major Robert Preston complained that fellow prosecutors had suppressed the FBI's documentation of abuse at the detention facility in Bagram, Afghanistan, and had suppressed and sometimes even destroyed detainee allegations of abuse and torture at Guantánamo, including those recorded in official FBI reports.[121] Capt. Carr accused Former Military Commission Chief Prosecutor, Colonel Fred Borch, of saying that the commission panels would be "handpicked and will not acquit these detainees."[122] Both Capt. Carr and Maj. Preston resigned, saying they could no longer "professionally, ethically or morally" participate in the military commission process.[123]

In October 2007, Colonel Morris Davis stepped down as chief prosecutor for the military commissions, citing political interference by Pentagon officials into decisions about "who we will charge, what we will charge, what evidence we will try to introduce, and how we will conduct a prosecution."[124] Prior to his resignation, Col. Davis filed a formal complaint against Brigadier General Thomas Hartmann, the legal advisor to the Defense Department's appointing authority for the military commissions. Col. Davis says that Brig. Gen. Hartmann pressured him to file cases that would attract media attention, despite the fact that those cases would require secretive, closed-door proceedings.[125] In February 2008, Col. Davis announced he will testify on behalf of detainee Salim Ahmed Hamdan, who plans to argue at a pretrial hearing that the alleged political interference cited by Col. Davis violates the MCA.[126] In March 2008, Col. Davis submitted papers for retirement from the military.[127]

agencies asking about the circumstances surrounding Slahi's interrogation.[128] When he finally expressed his concerns about interrogation methods in 2004, then-Chief Prosecutor Colonel Robert Swann countered that statements made under torture could be admitted during military commissions because the U.N. Convention Against Torture did not apply to those proceedings.[129] In addition, at that time, military commission rules did not prohibit the admission of evidence obtained by torture.

Eventually Lt. Col. Couch and a U.S. military Criminal Investigation Task Force agent concluded that Slahi had been tortured, following which Lt. Col. Couch withdrew from the prosecution. (See textbox above). "Here was somebody I felt was connected to September 11, but in our zeal to get information, we had compromised our ability to prosecute him," Lt. Col. Couch said. But Lt. Col. Couch has not completely given up on the possibility that

Slahi can be prosecuted. "I'm hoping there's some non-tainted evidence out there that can put the guy in the hole."[130]

Although military officials maintain that Slahi's statements have been corroborated by independent information, their reliability is still in dispute. Slahi described his responses to torture in a letter to his lawyers: "I yessed every accusation my [interrogators] made."[131] Prior to stepping down in October 2007, Former Chief Military Prosecutor Colonel Morris Davis stated that Slahi remains eligible for a military commission trial, but also acknowledged that concerns over Slahi's treatment raised by Lt. Col. Couch have delayed the prosecution.[132] Even if Slahi is never prosecuted, he could be detained indefinitely as an enemy combatant. And the decision to designate him as an enemy combatant presumably was made at least in part on the basis of his own coerced statements.

Binyam Mohamed

Binyam Mohamed

Binyam Mohamed reportedly was arrested in Karachi, Pakistan in April 2002. He was transferred to Guantánamo in September 2004, where he is currently held without charge.

Following his arrest in Pakistan, Mohamed maintains he was rendered to Morocco and then transferred to CIA custody in Afghanistan. He further states that he repeatedly lied in response to torture and abuse.[133]

Mohamed alleges that U.S. personnel in Pakistan suspended him from his cell with a leather strap tied around his wrists, barely permitting him to stand, and threatened him with physical abuse and rendition to countries where he could be tortured.[134] Mohamed's lawyer, Clive Stafford Smith, says the torture was documented by CIA officers who photographed Mohamed's injuries. In December 2007, Smith urged authorities to preserve the photos.[135]

During his detention in Morocco, Mohamed claims he was forbidden from going outside and never saw the sun; was hung by his ankles and beaten; had his penis mutilated; was subjected to loud music and noise, interrupting his sleep over the course of almost 18 months straight; and was forcibly administered drugs in apparent response to his hunger strike. In response to the torture, Mohamed says he attempted to tell his interrogators what he thought they wanted to hear, confessing falsely to some of their accusations.[136]

Mohamed says he was transferred to CIA custody in January 2004 and held at a detention facility in Kabul,

Afghanistan—known as the "Dark Prison"—until May 2004. CIA agents in Afghanistan allegedly subjected Mohamed to sensory deprivation, sleep deprivation and isolation; bombarded him with loud rap music and horror movie noises for almost three consecutive weeks; held him in complete darkness most of the day; and deprived him of food.[137] U.S. government interrogators in Afghanistan allegedly informed Mohamed that he and Jose Padilla were suspected of plotting to detonate a radioactive bomb in New York, and punished Mohamed when he did not confirm their version of events. Mohamed claims he was later told to sign a statement that included admissions regarding his alleged conspiracy with Padilla.[138] (See textbox above).

On December 5, 2005, John D. Altenburg, a retired Army major general and then-appointing authority for military commissions, referred charges against Mohamed for conspiring with al Qaeda members—including Osama bin Laden, Khalid Sheikh Mohammed, Abu Zubaydah and Jose Padilla—to attack civilians, attack civilian objects, commit murder, destroy property and commit acts of terrorism. The U.S. government alleged that Mohamed and Padilla conspired to construct a "dirty bomb," blow up high-rise apartment buildings, and blow up gas tankers to "free the prisoners in Cuba."[139] The charges against Mohamed were nullified when the Supreme Court struck down the first military commission process in *Hamdan*.

It is unclear whether the government has sufficient evidence to recharge Mohamed. Smith told Human Rights First: "There isn't a case against Binyam Mohamed unless they use torture evidence, whether it was tortured out of him or someone else."[140]

Additionally, in a December 2007 letter to the British Foreign Secretary David Milliband, Smith wrote: "I have been privy to materials that allegedly support the finding that Mr. Mohamed should be held. And while I cannot discuss some here (due to classification rules), I can state unequivocally that I have seen no evidence of any kind against Mr. Mohamed that is not the bitter fruit of torture."[141]

Disparate Courts, Disparate Treatment: The Case of Jose Padilla

Jose Padilla was arrested on a material witness warrant in June 2002 and held as an enemy combatant in military detention in Charleston, South Carolina, for more than three years. The initial allegations against Padilla were largely the same as those made against Mohamed in his military commission charge sheet, namely that the two men conspired to plant a dirty bomb and blow up buildings in the United States.[142]

Padilla was denied counsel for more than two years of his military detention. He also alleges that he was kept in stark isolation with virtually no human contact for prolonged periods and was physically abused. His claims of abuse include severe sensory deprivation and manipulation, and threats of rendition. He further alleges that he was shackled and manacled with a belly chain for hours in his cell, hooded and forced to stand in stress positions for long durations of time, threatened with execution and physical abuse, administered psychedelic drugs against his will, and often kept in complete darkness or in a bitterly cold room without a blanket.[143]

In June 2004, former Deputy Attorney General James Comey publicly announced Padilla's alleged involvement in the dirty bomb plot. Comey stated that Padilla's admissions in military custody would not be offered against him during a federal criminal trial. Nonetheless, Comey alleged that Padilla's statements were "heavily corroborated," "including by Padilla's new accomplice," who appears to have been Binyam Mohamed.[144] Despite Comey's representations, when Jose Padilla was finally transferred to civilian custody and criminally charged, the allegations against him bore no relationship to those described in the military commission charge sheet against Mohamed. Instead, Padilla was charged with materially supporting a North American terrorist cell that had no connection to the alleged dirty bomb plot.[145]

The government was forced to change course in Padilla's case when it filed charges against him in federal criminal court. In contrast to the military commission rules governing Mohamed's case, the introduction of involuntary statements is prohibited by federal constitutional law. (See Chapter 4, The Law). Prosecutors did not even attempt to introduce Padilla's admissions at his trial, nor did they seek to introduce any of Mohamed's statements, without which they apparently had no basis to proceed with charges regarding the "dirty bomb" plot.

On August 16, 2007, a jury convicted Padilla of all charges and in January 2008, he was sentenced to 17 years and 4 months in prison.

At this writing, prosecutors may be searching for untainted evidence against Mohamed in order to shore up their case. Mohamed's family reports having received recent visits from FBI agents, who asked questions about his arrest.[146] Whether or not prosecutors will succeed remains to be seen. In the meantime, the British government continues to engage in talks with U.S. authorities in an attempt to secure Mohamed's release.[147]

Even if Mohamed is never tried, he could be detained indefinitely as an enemy combatant, likely based in part on the statements he made under abuse. In addition, Mohamed's statements may play a role in other important military commission proceedings. The original charge sheet against him named eight co-conspirators, including Khalid Sheikh Mohammed. If Mohamed made statements under torture about any of these detainees, his statements may have been introduced during their CSRTs as a basis for detaining them. Given the MCA's rules on classified evidence, Mohamed's statements could also be introduced at their trials without calling Mohamed as a witness or even identifying him by name.

Omar Khadr

Omar Khadr

Omar Khadr, a twenty-one-year-old Canadian citizen, was detained at Bagram Air Base, Afghanistan, before being transferred to Guantánamo in October 2002.[148] He was 16 years old when he was taken to Guantánamo. Now in his sixth year of confinement, Khadr has spent more than a quarter of his life there.

In November 2007, Khadr was arraigned on charges of murder, attempted murder, providing material support for terrorism, and spying. He is accused of killing an American soldier with a hand grenade during combat with U.S. forces in Afghanistan in 2002.[149] If Khadr's trial proceeds, he will be the first juvenile in recent history to be tried for war crimes by any western nation, including the United States.

Khadr alleges he was repeatedly subjected to torture and cruel treatment during multiple interrogation sessions at Bagram and Guantánamo.[150] He states that military personnel in Bagram denied him pain medication for bullet wounds he sustained in battle with U.S. forces and that interrogators "tied his hands above the door frame and made him stand for hours at a time," "threw cold water on him," and "forced him to carry heavy buckets of water" while he was still recovering from his injuries. He also claims that interrogators kept him hooded, brought barking dogs into the interrogation room, threatened him with rape and transfer to other countries where he would be raped, and forbid him from using the bathroom, forcing him to urinate on himself.[151]

At Guantánamo, Khadr contends that interrogators forced him to lie on his stomach with his hands and feet shackled behind his back for hours at a time, making him urinate on himself, and that military police then dragged him through a mixture of urine and Pine Sol. Khadr further claims that he spent a month in isolation, confined to a room kept cold "like a refrigerator," and interrogators pulled his hair, spit in his face, repeatedly lifted him up and dropped him to the floor, and threatened him with extradition to countries where he would be raped. Interrogators also allegedly "short-shackled" his hands and feet to a bolt in the floor and threatened him with sexually violent acts.[152]. Short-shackling is the process of binding detainees at the wrist and ankle with metal or plastic handcuffs and then binding their wrists to their ankles while forcing them to lie on the ground or sit on the floor.

In a February 2008 affidavit, Khadr states: "I did not want to expose myself to any more harm, so I always just told interrogators what I thought they wanted to hear. Having been asked the same questions so many times, I knew what answers made interrogators happy and would always tailor my answers based on what I though would keep me from being harmed."[153]

Following the abuse, Khadr claims he "heard voices when no one was around," had a "persistent twitch ... on the left side of his face," and had "difficulty sleeping."[154] A psychological analysis of Khadr's conditions, conducted in March 2005, found "a high probability that he suffers from a significant mental disorder, including but not limited to post-traumatic stress disorder and depression. In addition, he appears to be having both delusions and hallucinations." The psychologist added that "Khadr's continued subjection to the threat of physical and mental abuse place him at significant risk for future psychiatric deterioration which may include irreversible psychiatric symptoms and disorders... ."[155]

What justice would look like in Khadr's case, and whether it can be achieved through a military commission trial, is the subject of much dispute. Khadr's lawyers argue that the MCA does not provide jurisdiction over juvenile cases and that killing an enemy soldier during armed combat does not even constitute a crime triable by military commission.[156] If Khadr is prosecuted at all, his lawyers say he should be tried in a civilian court pursuant to various safeguards designed to protect juveniles, as outlined in the Juvenile Justice Act.

Assuming, however, Khadr's dismissal motions on these grounds are denied, his trial is scheduled to begin sometime in 2008. Depending on the judge's definition of torture, the statements Khadr says he made under coercion may be admissible against him under the MCA. And the government has already signaled its intention to introduce Khadr's statements against him at trial. Court documents released in March 2008 reveal that the government has granted one of Khadr's interrogators immunity from prosecution for any abuse of Khadr in exhange for the interrogator's cooperation at trial.[157] The danger that Khadr could be convicted based at least in part on coerced evidence is compounded by other aspects of his case, including that prosecutors withheld an exculpatory witness from Khadr for months. In addition, defense lawyers claim that, during pretrial discovery, they were provided with an account of the firefight preceding Khadr's arrest that may have been altered to implicate Khadr.[158]

The Law

"But if force has been applied, this Court does not leave to local determination whether or not the confession was voluntary. There is torture of mind as well as body; the will is as much affected by fear as by force. And there comes a point where this Court should not be ignorant as judges of what we know as men."

– U.S. Supreme Court Justice Felix Frankfurter, *Watts v. Indiana*, 338 U.S. 49, 52 (1949)

U.S. Law Prohibits Coerced Confessions

The Due Process Clause to the U.S. Constitution secures the right to silence unless a criminal suspect "chooses to speak in the unfettered exercise of his own will."[159] This ban on coerced confessions is a hallmark of the U.S. criminal justice system. The Supreme Court has repeatedly held that due process prohibits the government's use of involuntary statements extracted through psychological pressure, physical intimidation, torture or other mistreatment.[160] The prohibition applies to self-incriminating confessions and to third-party statements.[161]

U.S. military law also excludes involuntary confessions, and it casts an even broader net than federal criminal law by prohibiting the introduction of any statements extracted through "the use of coercion, unlawful influence, or unlawful inducement."[162] The military's prohibition applies both to criminal trials by court-martial and to Geneva Convention Article 5 hearings, which are held during combat to determine whether to detain a prisoner as a POW or to refer the prisoner for a war crimes prosecution.[163]

In evaluating whether or not a confession was made voluntarily, federal courts consider the "totality of the circumstances" surrounding the interrogation, including the age, intelligence and education level of the accused; the length of the detention and interrogation; and the use of physical punishments such as the deprivation of food or sleep.[164] Federal courts have repeatedly excluded statements made following the use of various interrogation methods:

- solitary confinement or isolation,[165]
- sleep deprivation,[166]
- threats of death and physical harm,[167]
- beatings, and[168]
- nudity.[169]

Notably, some statements procured through the use of these very same techniques may be admissible under the MCA.[170]

The Supreme Court has repeatedly recognized that it is inconsistent with the justice system of any civilized society to permit the introduction of involuntary confessions. In *Rogers v. Richmond*, the Court stated that "ours is an accusatorial and not an inquisitorial system—a system in which the State must establish guilt by evidence independently and freely secured and may not by coercion prove its charge against an accused out of his own mouth."[171] The Court echoed this same view in *Jackson v. Denno* when it noted the "strongly felt attitude of our society that important human values are sacrificed where an agency of the government, in the course of securing a conviction, wrings a confession out of an accused against his will."[172] By excluding involuntary admissions, the Court explained, the law deters unlawful conduct, reflecting society's view "that in the end life and liberty can be as much endangered from illegal methods used to convict those thought to be criminals as from the actual criminals themselves."[173]

There are no emergency exceptions to the prohibition. "We are not impressed by the argument that law enforcement methods such as those under review are necessary to uphold our laws," the Court stated in *Chambers v. Florida*, upon evaluating an interrogation that included detention for five days and a final all-night session. "The Constitution proscribes such lawless means irrespective of the end."[174]

Coerced confessions are also excluded as unreliable.[175] But lack of reliability is a secondary concern. In fact, courts are prohibited from considering reliability or corroboration when evaluating claims of coercion. Where coercion is at issue, the Supreme Court has stated that evaluating admissibility based in part on a statement's veracity would be improper.[176] In a dissenting opinion now recognized as law, Justice Frankfurter warned: "This issue must be decided without regard to the confirmation of details in the confession by reliable other evidence. The determination must not be influenced by any irrelevant feeling of certitude that the accused is guilty of the crime to which he confessed."[177]

The MCA completely disregards this prohibition. On the one hand, it allows military commission judges to

consider the reliability and probative value of statements made under coercion. And on the other, it disables detainees from effectively challenging reliability or from proving that the abuse they endured amounted to torture. (See Chapter 2, The Policies and Practices).

Coerced Evidence Violates U.S. Treaty Obligations

International law prohibits the introduction of evidence procured by torture, or by cruel, inhuman or degrading treatment, in all legal proceedings. This prohibition is most clearly spelled out in the U.N. Convention Against Torture, which has been ratified by the United States. Article 15 provides: "Each State Party shall ensure that any statement which is established to have been made as a result of torture shall not be invoked as evidence in any proceedings, except against a person accused of torture as evidence that the statement was made."[178]

International law recognizes that excluding evidence extracted through torture deters future abuse. In its comments to the International Covenant on Civil and Political Rights (ICCPR), ratified by the United States in 1992,[179] the Human Rights Committee, a body of experts that interprets the ICCPR, states: "It is important for the discouragement of violations under Article 7 that the law must prohibit the use of admissibility in judicial proceedings of statements or confessions obtained through torture or other prohibited treatment."[180]

Common Article 3 of the Geneva Conventions also prohibits the admission of evidence obtained by torture, cruel treatment, or coercion. Specifically, it prohibits sentencing or executing defendants without a judgment from "a regularly constituted court affording all the judicial guarantees which are recognized as indispensable by civilized peoples."[181] The Supreme Court stated in *Hamdan* that the phrase, "all the judicial guarantees which are recognized as indispensable by civilized peoples," should be understood to encompass trial protections under customary international law, as reflected in Article 75 of Protocol I to the Geneva Conventions.[182] Among the rights set forth in Article 75 is the right not to be "compelled to testify against [one's] self or to confess guilt."[183] Thus, admission of coerced statements violates Common Article 3.

Prior to the enactment of the MCA, trying a detainee in violation of Common Article 3 constituted a federal war crime under U.S. statutory law.[184] In fact, following World War II, the U.S. government and its allies prosecuted several Japanese officers for their participation as judges and prosecutors in trials of U.S. service-members that relied on evidence extracted through torture.[185] The MCA, however, amended the federal War Crimes Act to limit the category of offenses that violate Common Article 3, and it excluded, in particular, the deprivation of a fair trial.[186] To the rest of the world, however, the admission of evidence derived from torture and other cruel treatment continues to constitute a war crime and a violation of international human rights obligations.

The Science and Results

"Maltreating the subject is from a strictly practical point of view as short-sighted as whipping a horse to his knees before a thirty-mile ride. It is true that almost anyone will eventually talk when subjected to enough physical pressures, but the information obtained in this way is likely to be of little intelligence value and the subject himself rendered unfit for further exploitation."

– Don Compos [pseudonym], "The Interrogation of Suspects Under Arrest," Studies in Intelligence, 2, no. 3, 1957

"Intense pain is quite likely to produce false confessions, concocted as a means of escaping from distress. A time-consuming delay results, while investigation is conducted and the admissions are proven untrue. During this respite the interrogatee can pull himself together. He may even use the time to think up new, more complex "admissions" that take still longer to disprove."

– CIA Training Manual, KUBARK Counterintelligence Interrogation (July 1965), p. 94

The military commission rules and CSRT procedures permitting the admission of coerced evidence are based on misguided assumptions about the reliability of statements extracted through coercion and abuse. Historical research on coercive interrogation techniques, scientific studies, and the experiences of law enforcement and government officials expose the flaws in these assumptions.

Scientific Studies Show Coercion Is Counterproductive

U.S. government scientists researched the effects of coercive interrogations following the "brainwashing" of American prisoners of war held by North Korea during the Korean War. A number of these prisoners praised the Communists and announced a desire to remain in North Korea.[187] Scientists discovered that techniques employed on a broad scale by communist forces were highly coercive and included isolation; semi-starvation and sleep deprivation; forcing prisoners to maintain stress positions, lean on sharp rocks and hold weights above their heads; putting prisoners in hangman's nooses; withholding needed medical care; threatening to harm prisoners' families; and instilling a fear of death, pain, or deformity.[188] The brutality stopped only when the prisoners "confessed" or otherwise cooperated with interrogators.[189]

American scientists determined that these methods induced compliance, but produced inaccurate and unreliable results.[190] They explained the effects with the moniker "DDD," which stands for debility, dependency and dread. The North Koreans sapped the prisoners of their physical strength; deprived them of basic necessities, thus increasing their dependency on their captors; and encouraged chronic fear by threatening the prisoners and their families. In almost all cases, the DDD approach led to total compliance.[191]

More recent reports on coercive interrogation techniques reach the same conclusions as the studies from the 1950s.[192] The Intelligence Science Board Study Report on Educing Information, Phase I (Intelligence Science Board Report), completed in 2006, is the most comprehensive scientific report on coercive interrogations to date. The report was sponsored by the Defense Intelligence Agency, the Intelligence Technology Information Center, and the Defense Department's Counterintelligence Field Activity. It examines all of the existing social and behavioral science studies on effective interrogation. These studies make a number of critical findings:

- Virtually no research on torture and other coercive interrogation techniques indicates that these techniques produce accurate, useful information from unwilling sources.[193]

- Most personal accounts and anecdotes of those subjected to torture and coercive interrogation techniques indicate they are not effective.[194]

- Stress and duress techniques adversely affect cognitive functioning, in particular the ability to recall and produce accurate and helpful information, making it difficult to elicit factual information.[195]

A number of the scientific papers included in the report support the conclusion that coercive interrogations are more likely to produce unreliable results.[196] In one study, Dr. Randy Borum explains that "[p]sychological theory and some (indirectly) related research suggest that coercion or pressure can actually increase a source's resistance and determination not to comply. Although pain is commonly assumed to facilitate compliance, there is no available scientific or systematic research to suggest that coercion can, will, or has provided accurate useful information from otherwise uncooperative sources."[197]

Similarly, in another paper, Col. Steven M. Kleinman reports that "the very means by which coercive methods undermine the source's resistance posture also may concomitantly degrade their ability to report the intelligence information they possess in a valid, comprehensive fashion."[198] In an interview, Col. Kleinman told Human Rights First: "There are two things you can obtain in the case of interrogation: compliance and cooperation...Compliance is forcing them to do something against their will. But to get [useful] information, you need to get some degree of cooperation. Ninety-nine percent of all the research Americans have done is about what people do to achieve compliance."[199]

The findings in the Intelligence Science Board Report are borne out by studies of the U.S. criminal justice system, which reveal a high correlation between false confessions and lengthy interrogations during which coercive techniques are used.[200] According to psychology Professor Saul Kassin, interrogators who employ coercive techniques may compel people to talk but they "are not nearly as good at determining if what they're getting is true or not."[201] False confessions, in turn, exert a powerful influence over prosecutors, judges, the media, and even defense attorneys, and they often lead to wrongful convictions. In fact, they may be "the most incriminating and persuasive false evidence of guilt" that the government brings to bear in a criminal case.[202] Some studies suggest that four out of five people (80 percent) who make false confessions and proceed to trial will likely be convicted—notwithstanding the presumption of innocence and the lack of reliable evidence corroborating their confessions.[203]

U.S. Adopts Communist Techniques

Most of the military and intelligence communities' scientific research on communist interrogation methods was conducted with the purpose of teaching U.S. government personnel to resist coercive interrogations, rather than to develop an understanding of how to inflict such coercion.[204] The research led to the creation in the 1950s of the U.S. Military's Survival, Evasion, Resistance, Escape (SERE) program, which prepares military personnel to survive coercive interrogation techniques such as waterboarding and stressful noises.[205] However, at least by the 1980s, the

CIA had begun developing "offensive techniques" based on the North Korean interrogation studies as well as its own experiments on interrogation. Also by the 1980s, CIA and Green Beret trainers reportedly began training Latin American militaries in similar techniques in places such as El Salvador, Guatemala, Ecuador, and Peru, and through its School of the Americas at Fort Benning, Georgia.[206]

It should come as no surprise, then, that the coercive interrogation methods outlined in the CIA manuals mirror the North Korean and Chinese techniques, including deprivation of sensory stimuli through solitary confinement or similar methods, threats of physical violence, and debility and pain.[207]

The CIA's own manuals warn against the misuse of coercive techniques, explaining that they can impair a subject's ability to accurately recall and communicate information, and may induce apathy and withdrawal.[208] Nonetheless, these same techniques have been repeatedly employed by the CIA, some U.S. military personnel, and even contractors on terrorist suspects in the last five years. (For comparison to Army Field Manual procedures, see textbox on right). Numerous credible media accounts have now made clear that U.S. military and CIA interrogators have used offensive techniques in pursuit of information from suspected terrorists, which strongly resemble or even come directly from SERE's defensive techniques.[209] Additionally, as shown in Chapter 3, many suspects have been detained for prolonged periods in conditions patently intended to create a DDD environment—the states of debility, dependency and dread.

Scientific Studies are Borne Out at Guantánamo

Just as coercive techniques proved unreliable during the Cold War, many experts believe they have failed to produce reliable intelligence from al Qaeda suspects in recent years.

Shortly after U.S. military interrogators began employing coercive interrogation tactics at Guantánamo, members of the FBI and the Pentagon's Criminal Investigative Task Force voiced their objections, contending that abusive techniques produced inaccurate intelligence.[210] In

U.S. Army Field Manual Prohibits Torture

In September 2006, the Pentagon issued a revised field manual on interrogation, Field Manual No. 2-22.3: Human Intelligence Collector Operations, which allows the use of nineteen specified procedures and prohibits eight others, including waterboarding, beatings and other forms of physical pain, induced hypothermia or heat injuries, forced nakedness, and deprivation of food, water and medical care.[211] The new manual states: "use of torture is not only illegal, but also it is a poor technique that yields unreliable results, may damage subsequent collection efforts, and can induce the source to say what he thinks the HUMINT [Human Intelligence] collector wants to hear. Use of torture can also have many possible negative consequences at national and international levels."[212] This language on reliability mirrors that of the Army's 1992 manual on interrogation, which also states that humane treatment leads to more effective interrogations.[213]

At a news briefing announcing the new field manual, Army Deputy Chief of Staff for Intelligence Lieutenant General John Kimmons said, "[n]o good intelligence is going to come from abusive practices. I think history tells us that. I think the empirical evidence of the last five years, hard years, tells us that."[214]

In February 2008, both houses of Congress passed legislation requiring all U.S. intelligence agents, including CIA interrogators, to adhere to the standards of interrogation outlined in the Army Field Manual. However, President Bush vetoed the bill on March 8, 2008.[215]

December 2003, an FBI email sent to FBI officials reported that the Military Liaison Defense Unit of the Bureau "has had a long standing and documented position against use of some of DOD's interrogation practices." These interrogations tactics, the email continued, "have produced no intelligence of a threat neutralization nature to date."[216]

FBI officials were further concerned that the interrogation methods employed by military personnel at Guantánamo were having an adverse impact on the FBI's own interrogations, disrupting the cooperative relationships agents were seeking to establish, and impeding the acquisition of useful and reliable information.[217] One FBI agent noted that he told high-level officials in the Justice Department's Criminal

Division of his concerns: "In my weekly meetings with DoJ, we often discussed DoD techniques and how they were not effective or producing Intel that was reliable."[218]

In an interview with Human Rights First, Jack Cloonan, a former FBI agent who interrogated various alleged al Qaeda members, stated that the abusive interrogations conducted at Guantánamo were "a complete and unmitigated failure."[219] Cloonan has also said that "any agent who walked into a room and saw a subject as has been described—crawled up in the fetal position, either deprived of water or subjected to unusually warm temperatures, pulling his hair out, people on hunger strikes, and so on—understands that that person is no good to you from an intelligence perspective. They've collapsed; they're not coherent. So what good is it?"[220]

Dr. Michael Gelles, the former chief psychologist for the Naval Criminal Investigation Service, also believes that coercive techniques were ineffective in eliciting cooperation at Guantánamo. Gelles has consulted with interrogators in Iraq, Afghanistan, and Guantánamo, and provided training on rapport-based approaches. According to Gelles, coercive tactics are used to "gather all the information you can and figure out later" what is true and what is false. At Guantánamo, says Dr. Gelles, coercive methods "distorted information" and turned parts of the intelligence community into "a dog chasing its tail."[221] Dr. Gelles' comments echo Col. Kleiman's: "'If the goal is to get information, then using coercive techniques may be effective. But if the goal is to get reliable and accurate information, looking at this adversary, rapport-building is the best approach,'" said Gelles.[222] (See textbox below). In place of coercion, the FBI advocates a rapport-building approach.[223]

The FBI Weighs In: Due Process Facilitates Interrogation

Former FBI agent Dan Coleman, who interrogated numerous al Qaeda members during his career, maintains that providing the same legal rights afforded in regular criminal cases—including defense counsel—is crucial to eliciting useful and reliable information from terrorist suspects. "'The lawyers show these guys there's a way out," says Coleman. "It's human nature. People don't cooperate with you unless they have some reason to. ... Brutalization doesn't work. We know that. Besides, you lose your soul.'"[224]

Former FBI agent Jack Cloonan, who also interrogated many al Qaeda members as part of the FBI team assigned to the bin Laden unit, similarly insists that a legal and humane approach is the best method for obtaining reliable information. In interviews with Human Rights First, Cloonan asserted that exposing al Qaeda members to due process, including access to counsel, created "extremely positive results." "They expected torture," explains Cloonan, but "[t]hey were amazed at the very concept of due process. A tremendous amount of information came our way as a result of treating people humanely."[225]

The Consequences

"The features and products of coerced confessions, and before them, trials by fire and water, have been viewed by advancing civilization as inherently flawed. There is nothing to persuade us that we should go back a few hundred years in our judicial history to learn again the lessons of disgraced chapters in that history."

— Brigadier General James P. Cullen (U.S. Army Reserve JAG Corps, (ret.), former Chief Judge (IMA), U.S. Army Court of Criminal Appeals), interview by Human Rights First, April 12, 2007

A question of legitimacy hangs over the detention and legal proceedings at Guantánamo. Defense lawyers and human rights groups are not alone in their indictment of the military commission process. Many law enforcement and military officials are critical of the MCA's evidentiary rules. These officials know that the reliance on coerced testimony will only serve to tarnish the image of the military commission proceedings at home and in the international community, jeopardize the government's ability to secure convictions that can withstand scrutiny on appeal, and perpetuate the use of abusive interrogation techniques.

Interview with Former Military Commissions Official

Human Rights First has interviewed a source (for convenience, assigned here a male gender) who formerly worked on detainee prosecutions at the Office of Military Commissions. The source agreed to speak to Human Rights First in part because he is deeply conflicted about the upcoming military commission trials. On the one hand, he is firmly committed to prosecuting suspected terrorists. On the other hand, he believes that such prosecutions should not be based on unreliable and illegal evidence. Our source told Human Rights First that many of the cases identified for military commission trials rely almost entirely on detainee admissions. In fact, he says that over 90 percent of the evidence collected against any given detainee is testimonial. As a result, the success or failure of the trials will hinge on the admissibility and credibility of detainee statements. The introduction of coerced statements— made either by defendants or third-party witnesses—puts successful prosecution in jeopardy.

Our source reports that military commission prosecutors investigating the detainees cannot themselves know the full extent to which testimonial evidence is tainted by abuse because intelligence personnel have withheld information about sources and the interrogation methods used. Indeed, in the wake of the 2004 Abu Ghraib scandal, military commission prosecutors were affirmatively prohibited from inquiring about the possible abuse of detainees they sought to prosecute or use as witnesses. According to our source, the explanation for this prohibition was that such inquiries might impede abuse investigations.

Our source is familiar with a 2004 memorandum, proposing standard operating procedures for commission prosecutors, which was provided to the chief military commission prosecutor. Human Rights First does not have a copy of the memorandum, but the source summarized it as follows: It noted that prosecutors had received incomplete information from military interrogators and several federal agencies, including the CIA and the Defense Intelligence Agency, regarding the capture and internment of detainees. It further stated that the CIA had failed to respond to requests for information, prosecutors had been denied access to agencies' legal opinions regarding the treatment of detainees, and detainee statements to law enforcement officials alleging abuse were incomplete.

The memorandum made the following recommendations: (1) Detainees who have been subjected to coercive interrogation methods should not be charged unless prosecutors are provided with all documents generated about the detainees, including interrogation plans and logs and classified and unclassified reports; (2) All statements of the accused should be provided to defense counsel, whether or not these statements are considered exculpatory; (3) All memoranda and any documents regarding interrogation plans should be provided to defense counsel; (4) Defense counsel should receive notice of any statements obtained by coercive means; and (5) Prosecutors should seek complete copies of all legal memoranda created by government agencies concerning interrogation techniques that have been employed.[226]

Law Enforcement and Military Officials Weigh In

FBI personnel were primarily assigned to Guantánamo as part of the Criminal Investigation Task Force (CITF), an inter-agency operation set up to investigate individuals suspected of war crimes and terrorist acts.[227] Initially, CITF worked alongside the Army's Joint Task Force170 (JTF-170), the military intelligence unit assigned to Guantánamo.[228] But the military's abusive tactics ultimately compelled CITF officials to separate law enforcement from intelligence operations.[229]

In November 2002, FBI agents reviewed a version of JTF-170's proposed interrogation techniques and concluded that many of them were prohibited by the U.S. Constitution.[230] They also found that many of the techniques could constitute torture under U.S. law, subjecting interrogators to possible criminal prosecution. Finally, they concluded that statements extracted through these techniques would not be admissible in U.S. courts, even if they could be admitted during military commission trials.[231] (See textbox above).

On December 14, 2002, Major General Geoffrey Miller, then-commander of all Guantánamo operations, presented CITF with standard operating procedures for the use of reverse-engineered SERE techniques on detainees. CITF protested that the techniques were illegal, regardless of whether Maj. Gen. Miller or anyone else had authorized them, and prohibited its interrogators from participating in or even observing interrogations using those methods.[232] According to Colonel Brittain P. Mallow, then-CITF commander, the law enforcement community's view on the abusive interrogations authorized at Guantánamo was as follows:

> No. 1, it's not going to work ... No. 2, if it does work, it's not reliable. No. 3, it may not be legal, ethical or moral. No. 4, it's going to hurt you when you have to prosecute these guys. No. 5, sooner or later, all of this stuff is going to come to light, and you're going to be embarrassed.[233]

Numerous senior military officials—both active duty and retired—also contend that the use of coercive interrogation techniques has jeopardized the government's ability to proceed with prosecutions and secure convictions. In December 2002, Former Navy General Counsel Alberto Mora urged Defense Department General Counsel William Haynes "not to rely" on CITF memoranda authorizing abusive techniques as they were "almost certainly not reflective of conscious policy."[234] "The memos, and the practices they authorized," Mora recalls informing Haynes, "threatened the entire military commission process."[235]

Some law enforcement and military experts also believe that the MCA's provisions on coerced evidence will only perpetuate the use of cruel interrogation tactics. Jack Cloonan, a former FBI agent who interrogated many al

Qaeda members, has said: "You cannot give an agent or an investigator an open-ended invitation to use coercive interrogation tactics to get information... .It's the slippery slope because god knows where it will end up taking you. To keep everybody on the up and up you don't allow that— you get bad information, unreliable sometimes, [and] serious consequences to the reputation of the organization and the United States."[236]

Finally, many military officials have expressed grave concerns about the perception, at home and abroad, of the upcoming military commission trials. James P. Cullen, a retired Brigadier General in the U.S. Army Reserve Judge Advocate General's Corps, states that the MCA "approach is doomed to failure because a trial conducted under such rules is fundamentally incapable of producing credible results, and tarnishes our whole justice system."[237] Brig. Gen. Cullen still believes prosecutions are the right course of action, but adds: "If we plan on trying people, as I think we should, we can only use interrogation methods that will stand up in court and will pass public muster, here and elsewhere."[238]

FBI Believed Coercive Tactics May Jeopardize Future Trial Testimony

In the immediate aftermath of the September 11 attacks, the CIA reportedly requested FBI assistance in interrogating terrorism suspects in Afghanistan and elsewhere. For security reasons, the CIA did not want its own agents to appear in court and hoped that FBI agents could testify about information acquired during the interrogations.[239] FBI officials reportedly cautioned that its participation in abusive interrogation sessions could jeopardize future prosecutions and ruin the agency's credibility.[240]

FBI Director Robert Mueller was asked at a Congressional hearing in May 2004 whether the FBI had prohibited its agents from participating in interrogations conducted by the CIA because of the abusive methods employed. Director Mueller replied: "My understanding is that there are standards that have been established by others legally that may well be different from the FBI standards, and if that were the case and there were a departure from the FBI standards, we were not to participate." Mueller took great pains not to accuse the CIA or the Defense Department's interrogators of crimes. But he did state that "it is the FBI's policy to prohibit interrogation by force, threats of force or coercion. Where we have conducted interviews, we have adhered to that policy."

He further explained that the FBI's standards for interrogation were "based on our belief on what is effective, our belief on what is appropriate, our belief on—and part of the footing of that is, quite obviously, the fact that we would have to testify in court on standards of voluntariness and the like."[241]

Conclusion and Recommendations

Congress passed the MCA in 2006 under pressure from the Bush Administration to make accommodations for the CIA's use of harsh interrogation techniques. Rather than repudiate the CIA's methods, or even accept the inadmissibility of statements obtained through torture and other cruel treatment, the Bush Administration sought to use the commission process to legitimize the CIA's program. In so doing, it created a second tier of justice—one that threatens the successful prosecutions of those allegedly responsible for the September 11 attacks and ignores deeply-held American principles of due process.

As the military commission proceedings gather momentum in 2008, the American public and the international community will be watching. It is past time to correct the misguided embrace of torture and coercive interrogation techniques. To restore integrity to the American justice system, Human Rights First makes the following recommendations.

Criminal Trials

- The U.S. government should try terrorist suspects by court-martial or in civilian criminal courts where coerced confessions are inadmissible, the introduction of hearsay evidence is restricted to protect reliability, and the rules governing the disclosure and introduction of classified evidence are clear. Trying suspects in civilian courts or courts-martial pursuant to these fair trial standards will:

  - Restore the focus of the proceedings to the crimes committed by the accused;

  - Ensure our government's ability to secure convictions that can survive on appeal;

  - Decrease the risk of wrongful convictions based on the use of false confessions;

  - Discourage the use of torture and coercive interrogation techniques; and

  - Legitimize the proceedings in the eyes of the international community.

- In the alternative, Congress should amend the Military Commissions Act to:

  - Prohibit during criminal trials the introduction of evidence obtained through coercion or cruel, inhuman or degrading treatment;

  - Prohibit convictions based on confessions alone and require corroborating evidence of every offense charged;

  - Impose additional discovery requirements on government prosecutors, subject to the same procedures employed in U.S. courts for potentially classified evidence. Without such discovery, defense lawyers will have little basis for objecting to the introduction of coerced statements. These discovery requirements should include the classified sources, methods and activities by which statements were obtained. This information may be derived from:

    (1) confinement records, investigative reports, and interrogation plans and logs revealing the abuse and/or alleged abuse of the suspect and/or government witnesses;

(2) the names and locations of all witnesses present during interrogations;

(3) access to prosecution witnesses who may have been abused; and

- Require the government to prove the reliability and materiality of hearsay evidence it seeks to introduce.

Detention Hearings

- The U.S. government should prohibit the admission of statements extracted through torture or coercion during detention hearings. If CSRTs are upheld as constitutional, CSRT procedures should be amended to that effect.

- Congress should require the U.S. government to provide counsel to detainees at detention hearings who can identify and object to evidence that may be the product of coercion.

- Congress should restore habeas corpus rights to detainees designated as enemy combatants. Restoring habeas corpus rights will enable Article 3 judges to examine whether detention decisions have been made based on coerced evidence.

Investigation and Interrogation

- The U.S. government should require government intelligence agents to adhere to the standards of interrogation outlined in the U.S. Army Field Manual. Forbidding the use of torture and cruel treatment will deter future abuse and reduce the likelihood of admitting false confessions or statements obtained by cruel treatment or coercion.

- Congress should require the videotaping of interrogations of terrorist suspects that are conducted away from the battlefield. Recording interrogations will permit thorough judicial review of abuse allegations, deter future abuse, and reduce the likelihood of admitting false confessions or statements obtained by cruel treatment or coercion.

Failure to take these steps now will result in precisely the situation feared by one source who formerly worked at the Office of Military Commissions: "If we fast forward 50 years from now, two things will become clear" says the source. "One, we compromised our ideals as Americans. Two, by compromising those ideals, we may have compromised our ability to bring to justice those al Qaeda operatives responsible for September 11."[242]

Appendices

A. Glossary of Terms

ARB	Administrative Review Board
BAU	FBI Behavioral Analysis Unit
CAT	U.N. Convention Against Torture
CIA	Central Intelligence Agency
CID	Cruel, Inhuman or Degrading Treatment
CITF	Criminal Investigative Task Force at Guantánamo
CSRT	Combatant Status Review Tribunal
DDD	Debility, Dependency and Dread
DoD	Department of Defense
DoJ	Department of Justice
DTA	Detainee Treatment Act of 2005
FBI	Federal Bureau of Investigation
HUMINT	Human Intelligence
ICCPR	International Covenant on Civil and Political Rights
JTF-170	Army's Joint Task Force at Guantánamo
MCA	Military Commissions Act of 2006
OLC	Department of Justice, Office of Legal Counsel
OMC	Office of Military Commissions
POW	Prisoner of War
SERE	U.S. Military's Survival, Evasion, Resistance, Escape Program

B. The Numbers

Visual breakdown of Human Rights First's findings

Table starts next page.

B. The Numbers
Visual breakdown of Human Rights First's findings

This chart lists the names of detainees who allege they were abused in custody. It also lists the names of detainees against whom coerced evidence may be used, or already may have been used, during detention hearings and military commission trials. It does not necessarily include the names of all detainees who were abused. The U.S. government continues to withhold as classified the interrogation techniques used against most detainees. In addition, the chart relies in large part on attorney statements of detainee abuse and transcripts from CSRT and ARB hearings; however, most detainees do not have legal representation, and some chose not to participate in their detention hearings, leaving them with no outlet for describing the abuse they may have endured. Even those detainees who did participate in their hearings may have withheld details of their treatment because they were afraid those disclosures would result in further abuse. For example, several detainees, such as Abdul Aziz Saad Al Khaldi and Muhammad Ismail, refused to participate in their hearings until military commission officials guaranteed that their participation would not lead to future abuse.

Reference Key	
Acronym	Definition
HVD	High Value Detainee
CSRT	Combatant Status Review Tribunal
ARB	Administrative Review Board
MC	Military Commission
*	Detainee Charged by Military Commission

Name of Detainee	Confirmed Abuse and Allegations of Abuse	Who Detainee Implicated or May Have Implicated	Who Implicated Detainee or May Have Implicated Detainee	Source of Information
Abd al-Hadi al-Iraqi, HVD	Detainee was likely subjected to enhanced interrogation techniques. The Bush administration confirmed that the detainee was held in secret CIA custody.			Mark Benjamin, "The CIA's Latest 'Ghost Detainee,'" *Salon*, May 22, 2007; Human Rights Watch, "US: Close CIA Prisons Still in Operation," April 27, 2007; Office of the Assistant Secretary of Defense (Public Affairs), "Defense Department Takes Custody of a High-Value Detainee," Department of Defense news release, April 27, 2007.
Abd Al Malik al Wahab (aka Abdulmalik Abdulwahhab Al-Rahabi), No. 037	Detainee alleges he was beaten, interrogated with a gun to his head, had his head rubbed against the concrete until he lost consciousness, sleep deprived, made to wear only shorts, made to sleep on a thin mat, exposed to extreme temperatures, given inadequate medical care, sprayed with "disorienting gas," and threatened with violence to his family, torture, rape, and transfer to a country where he may be tortured.	Himself	Mohammed al-Qahtani	CSRT Set 4, p. 433-446; Letter from Marc D. Falkoff to Administrative Review Board, "Re: ARB Hearing for Abd al Malik Abd al Wahab, ISN 037," April 30, 2005 (on file with Human Rights First); The New York Center for Constitutional Rights (CCR), "Report on Torture, Cruel, Inhuman, and Degrading Treatment of Prisoners at Guantánamo Bay, Cuba," July 2006; Frank Davies, "Terror Court Unveils Lives of the Accused," *Miami Herald*, November 14, 2004.
Abd al Nasir Muhammad Abd Al Qadir Khantumani, No. 307	Detainee alleges he was tortured and beaten in Pakistan with US forces present.	Himself		CSRT Set 51, p. 3634-3643.

Name of Detainee	Confirmed Abuse and Allegations of Abuse	Who Detainee Implicated or May Have Implicated	Who Implicated Detainee or May Have Implicated Detainee	Source of Information
Abd Al Rahim Abdul Rassak Janko, No. 489	Detainee alleges he was beaten and tortured in a Taliban prison in Kandahar.	Himself		CSRT Set 51, p. 3620-3633; ARB Set 18, p. 23143-23158.
Abd al-Rahim al-Nashiri (aka Abd al Rahil Gysseub Nygannad Abdu; Mullah Bilal; Bilal; Abu Bilal al-Makki; Khalid al Safani; Amm Ahmad), HVD, No. 10015	The Bush administration acknowledges that CIA interrogators waterboarded the detainee. The administration has also confirmed the use of "alternative" interrogation techniques on the detainee while in secret CIA custody. The detainee further alleges he was "tortured" by Americans.	Himself	Jamal Ahmed Mohammed Ali Al-Badawi (al-Nashiri believes Al-Badawi was tortured into confessing in another country; Al-Badawi is currently on the FBI's most wanted list)	Brian Ross and Richard Esposito, "CIA's Harsh Interrogation Techniques Described," *ABC News*, November 18, 2005; President George W. Bush, "President Discusses Creation of Military Commissions to Try Suspected Terrorists," White House news release, September 6, 2006; CIA Director Michael Hayden, Senate (Select) Intelligence Committee, Current and Projected National Security Threats, 110th Cong., 2ⁿ Sess., 2008; CSRT, http://www.defenselink.mil/news/transcript_ISN10015.pdf; Lesley Clark, "Terrorism suspect says he lied to stop torture," *Miami Herald*, March 31, 2007.
Abd al-Salam ali al-Hila, No. 1463	Detainee alleges he was sleep deprived and kept in the Dark Prison, chained to the wall and subjected to constant noise.	Himself		Unclassified Summary of Evidence for ARB, http://www.dod.mil/pubs/foi/detainees/csrt_arb/ARB_Round_2_Factors_900-1009.pdf#88; Carlotta Gall, "Rights Group Reports Afghanistan Torture," *New York Times*, December 19, 2005; Human Rights Watch, "U.S. Operated Secret 'Dark Prison' in Kabul," December 19, 2005.
Abdul Aziz Saad Al Khaldi, No. 112	Detainee alleges he was physically and psychologically tortured.	Himself		CSRT Set 31, p. 2197-2207.
Abdul Majid Muhammed, No. 555	Detainee alleges he was captured by Afghans, hit in the lip with a gun and denied food for one week.			CSRT Set 31, p. 2251-2265; ARB Set 7, p. 20586-20593.
Abdullah Al Tayabi, No. 332	Detainee alleges that, at a prison in Kabul, he was beaten and interrogators threatened to kill him. At Bagram, detainee alleges interrogators put a gun to his face and threatened to kill him, threw him on the ground and dragged him by his legs, bound his hands and feet for seven to nine days, and subjected him to sleep deprivation. In Kandahar, detainee alleges US soldiers stripped him and tied him up in the rain for three hours and kicked him. Detainee further alleges that, at Guantánamo, he was hit, shackled and had his medication withheld.	Himself		CSRT Set 49 -50, p. 3378-3397.

Name of Detainee	Confirmed Abuse and Allegations of Abuse	Who Detainee Implicated or May Have Implicated	Who Implicated Detainee or May Have Implicated Detainee	Source of Information
Abu Faraj al-Libi (aka al-Uzayti; Mahfuz; Abd al-Hafiz; Abu Hamada; Tawfiq), HVD, No. 10017	The Bush administration has confirmed the use of "alternative" interrogation techniques on the detainee while in secret CIA custody.			Brian Ross and Richard Esposito, "CIA's Harsh Interrogation Techniques Described," *ABC News*, November 18, 2005; President George W. Bush, "President Discusses Creation of Military Commissions to Try Suspected Terrorists," White House news release, September 6, 2006.
Abu Zubaydah (aka Zayn al-Abidin; Hani; Tariq), HVD, No. 10016	The Bush administration acknowledges that CIA interrogators waterboarded the detainee. The administration has also confirmed the use of "alternative" interrogation techniques on the detainee while in secret CIA custody.	Himself; Ibrahim Mahdy Achmed Zeidan; Khalid Sheikh Mohammed; Ramzi Bin al-Shibh; Jose Padilla (charged in federal court)	Binyam Mohamed; Jose Padilla (charged in federal court); Mohammed Harkat (charged in Canada); Adil Charkaoui (charged in Canada)	CSRT, http://www.defenselink.mil/news/transcript_ISN10016.pdf; Human Rights First, "Military Commissions in Context as Guantanamo Enters Its Fifth Year," *Human Rights First Blog*, February 28, 2006; Douglas Jehl and Eric Lichtblau "Shift on Suspect is Linked to Role of Qaeda Figures," *New York Times*, November 24, 2005; "New Intelligence Report on New Generation of Terrorists; Clinton Defends Efforts to Get Bin Laden; Venezuela's Foreign Minister Angry at Airport Detention," CNN Transcript, September 24, 2006; CIA Director Michael Hayden, Senate (Select) Intelligence Committee, Current and Projected National Security Threats, 110th Cong., 2- Sess., 2008; President George W. Bush, "President Discusses Creation of Military Commissions to Try Suspected Terrorists," White House news release, September 6, 2006; Ibrahim Zeidan's CSRT Set 11, p.1171-1178; Amanda Ripley, "The Case of the Dirty Bomber," *Time*, June 16, 2002; Michael Isikoff and Mark Hosenball, "Tainted Evidence: Canada tosses CIA terror testimony obtained through waterboarding," *Newsweek*, March 5, 2008.
Adnan Farhan Abdul Latif, No. 156	Detainee alleges he was visited by an "Immediate Reaction Force" team that sprayed him with pepper spray, beat him and put his head in the toilet. Detainee alleges that, following his arrival at Guantánamo, he was hit, kicked, questioned with a gun to his head, kept in an open-air cage and forced to wear only shorts, thus preventing him from praying.			Richard Serrano, "Guantanamo Bay Justice," *Los Angeles Times*, November 7, 2004; The Talking Dog Blog Interview with Marc Falkoff, March 30, 2007; Mark Falkoff, "Poems from Guantanamo," *Amnesty International USA*, Fall 2007.

Name of Detainee	Confirmed Abuse and Allegations of Abuse	Who Detainee Implicated or May Have Implicated	Who Implicated Detainee or May Have Implicated Detainee	Source of Information
*Ahmed Khalfan Ghailani (aka Haytham al-Kini), HVD, No. 10012	The Bush administration has confirmed the use of "alternative" interrogation techniques on the detainee while in secret CIA custody.			CSRT, http://www.defenselink.mil/news/transcript_ISN10012.pdf; Brian Ross and Richard Esposito, "CIA's Harsh Interrogation Techniques Described," *ABC News*, November 18, 2005; President George W. Bush, "President Discusses Creation of Military Commissions to Try Suspected Terrorists," White House news release, September 6, 2006.
*Ahmed Muhammed Haza Al-Darbi, No. 768	Detainee alleges a U.S. interrogator at Bagram beat and kicked him, forced him to remove his pants, and left him hanging from his handcuffs.	Himself		Unclassified Summary of Evidence for CSRT, http://www.dod.mil/pubs/foi/detainees/csrt_arb/000600-000699.pdf#8; Tim Golden, "In Final Trial, G.I. Is Acquitted Of Abusing Afghan Detainees," *New York Times*, June 2, 2006; Michael Melia, Associated Press, "Abuse claims complicating Gitmo trials," *Miami Herald*, March 14, 2008.
*Ali Abd al-Aziz Ali (aka Ammar al-Baluchi), HVD, No. 10018	The Bush administration has confirmed the use of "alternative" interrogation techniques on the detainee while in secret CIA custody.		Khalid Sheikh Mohammed	CSRT, http://www.defenselink.mil/news/transcript_ISN10018.pdf; President George W. Bush, "President Discusses Creation of Military Commissions to Try Suspected Terrorists," White House news release, September 6, 2006; Substitution for the Testimony of Khalid Sheikh Mohammed, Defendant's Exhibit 941, *U.S. v. Moussaoui*, C.R. No. 01-455-A.
Ali al-Hajj al-Sharqawi, No. 1457	Detainee alleges he was rendered to Jordan, where he was tortured and interrogated for two years, and threatened with sexual abuse and electrocution. Detainee alleges that, during his transfer to a CIA proxy prison in Kabul, his clothes were removed, his body was searched, his handcuffs were tied to the walls, his hands and feet were tied together, and he was picked up like a sack and thrown on top of another prisoner. Detainee alleges that, at Guantánamo, an interrogator threatened to return him to Jordan.	Himself		Human Rights Watch, "Double Jeopardy: CIA Renditions to Jordan," April 2008.
Aziz Abdul Naji, No. 744	Detainee alleges he was tortured and beaten.	Himself		CSRT Set 50, p. 3476-3477; ARB Set 1, p. 1014-1015.
Baidullah Bertola Obaidullah, No. 762	Detainee alleges he was threatened with a knife, had his hands bound and sandbags tied to his arms and was subjected to sleep deprivation.	Himself; Bostan Karim		CSRT Set 42, p. 2769-2779; ARB Set 8, p. 20970-20981; Bostan Karim CSRT Set 31, p. 2221-2227; Bostan Karim ARB Set 10, p. 21489-21501.

Name of Detainee	Confirmed Abuse and Allegations of Abuse	Who Detainee Implicated or May Have Implicated	Who Implicated Detainee or May Have Implicated Detainee	Source of Information
Binyam Mohamed, No. 1458	Detainee alleges that, while detained in Morocco, he was hung by his ankles, beaten, cut with a scalpel, subjected to loud noise, and forcibly given drugs. In CIA custody in Kabul, detainee alleges he was sensory deprived, sleep deprived, held in isolation, subjected to loud noise for almost three weeks, kept in complete darkness, and deprived of food.	Himself; Abu Zubaydah; Khalid Sheikh Mohammed; Jose Padilla (charged in federal prison)	Jose Padilla (charged in federal prison)	David Rose, "M16 and CIA 'Sent Student to Morocco to be Tortured," *Guardian (UK)*, December 11, 2005; Motion to Suppress Physical Evidence and Issue Writs of Testficandum, *U.S. v. Padilla*, No. 04-60001- (S.D.Fla Oct. 04, 2006); Douglas Jehl and Eric Lichtblau "Shift on Suspect is Linked to Role of Qaeda Figures," *New York Times*, November 24, 2005; Carol Rosenberg, "Lawyer seeks Britain's help in preserving Guantanamo evidence," *Miami Herald*, December 10, 2007; Brief of Binyam Mohammed as Amicus Curiae in Support of Petitioner, *Hamdan v. Rumsfeld*, 126 S. Ct. 2749 (2006), (No. 05-184); Memorandum from Attorney Clive Stafford Smith, "Binyam Mohammed al-Habashi."
Bostan Karim, No. 975	Detainee alleges he was sleep deprived in U.S. custody at Bagram. Detainee further alleges that he was tied very tightly en route to Guantánamo.		Baidullah Bertola Obaidullah	CSRT Set 31, p. 2221-2227; ARB Set 10, p. 21489-21501.
Boudella al Hajj, No. 10006	Detainee alleges he was shackled at his hands and feet, had his mouth taped, and had his eyes bandaged for four days on his way to Guantánamo.			CSRT Set 7, p. 767-791.
Fahed Nasser Mohamed, No. 013	Detainee alleges he was tortured by Afghans.	Himself		CSRT Set 50, p. 3462-3466; ARB Set 2, p. 624-629.
Fahd Umr Abd Al Majid Al Sharif, No. 215	Detainee alleges he was tortured and beaten in Kandahar.	Himself		CSRT Set 42, p. 2740-2751; ARB Set 17, p. 22855-22866.
Farooq Ali Ahmed, No. 032			Mohammed al-Qahtani	Corine Hegland, "Guantanamo's Grip," *National Journal*, February 3, 2006; Letter from Marc D. Falkoff to Administrative Review Board, "Re: ARB Hearing for Faruq Ali Ahmed, ISN 032," February 5, 2005 (on file with Human Rights First).
Gouled Hassan Dourad (aka Guleed Hassan Ahmad; Hamad), HVD, No. 10023	The Bush administration has confirmed the use of "alternative" interrogation techniques on the detainee while in secret CIA custody.			Brian Ross and Richard Esposito, "CIA's Harsh Interrogation Techniques Described," *ABC News*, November 18, 2005; President George W. Bush, "President Discusses Creation of Military Commissions to Try Suspected Terrorists," White House news release, September 6, 2006.
Ha Il Aziz Ahmed Al Maythali, No. 840	Detainee alleges he was tortured and his testicles were disfigured in a Karachi prison.	Himself		CSRT Set 31, p. 2156-2158.

Name of Detainee	Confirmed Abuse and Allegations of Abuse	Who Detainee Implicated or May Have Implicated	Who Implicated Detainee or May Have Implicated Detainee	Source of Information
Hassan Bin Attash, No. 1456	Detainee alleges that, while held in a Karachi jail, Pakistani and American interrogators hit and kicked him. Detainee further alleges that, while in custody in Jordan, he was tortured, sleep deprived, slapped, hung upside down, beaten on the soles of his feet, and threatened with electric shocks.	Himself		Farah Stockman, "7 Detainees Report Transfer to Nations That Use Torture," *Boston Globe*, April 26, 2006; Amnesty International USA, "'Your confessions are ready for you to sign': Detention and torture of political suspects;" Human Rights Watch, "Double Jeopardy: CIA Renditions to Jordan," April 2008.
Ibrahim Mahdy Achmed Zeidan, No. 761	Detainee alleges he was captured by Afghans that were part of the official government and that they "tortured" him and treated him "very badly."		Abu Zubaydah; Anwar Abu Faris (captured and interrogated in Jordan; Zeidan believes Faris was tortured)	CSRT Set 11, p. 1171-1178.
*Ibrahim Mahmoud Al Qosi, No. 54	Detainee alleges his hands and feet were tied behind him, guards stepped on his bare back with boots as they roped him up, he was dragged into the interrogation room where he developed lacerations where the ropes hit his skin, he was strapped to the floor and wrapped in an Israeli flag while being shown pornographic pictures, he was sexually humiliated by practices that included guards having sex in his presence and female interrogators rubbing their bodies against him, he was left in a refrigerated interrogation room for a long time with constant deafening music, he was stripped of items such as water, a toothbrush and the Koran, and interrogators threatened to turn the detainee over to the secret police of countries known to use torture.	Himself		*Ibrahim Ahmed Mahmoud Al Qosi v. George W. Bush et. al.* USDCDC Petition for Writ of Mandamus and/or Writ of Habeas Corpus, and Complaint for Declaratory, Injunctive and Other Relief; Unclassified Summary of Evidence for CSRT, http://www.dod.mil/pubs/foi/detainees/csrt_arb/000001-000100.pdf#65.
Jaralleh Al-Marri, No. 334	Detainee alleges that, while at Bagram, he was beaten, hit with a 2x4, threatened with death, and shortshackled.			Talking Dog Blog Interview with Jonathan Hafetz, April 16, 2006.
Khaled Qasim, No. 242	Detainee made conflicting statements during his CSRT hearing, switching between allegations that he had been "tortured" and "mistreated."	Himself		CSRT Set 53, p. 3936-3939; ARB Set 1, p.975-976.

Name of Detainee	Confirmed Abuse and Allegations of Abuse	Who Detainee Implicated or May Have Implicated	Who Implicated Detainee or May Have Implicated Detainee	Source of Information
*Khalid Sheikh Mohammed (aka Mukhtar; KSM), HVD, No. 10024	The Bush administration acknowledges that CIA interrogators waterboarded the detainee. The administration has also confirmed the use of "alternative" interrogation techniques on the detainee while in secret CIA custody.	Himself; Mohd Farik bin Amin; Majid Khan; Riduan bin Isomuddin; Walid bin Attash; Ramzi Bin al-Shibh; Mustafa Ahmed al-Hawsawi; Ali Abd al-Aziz Ali; Mohammed al Qahtani; Ali Saleh Khallah al-Marri (charged in federal court); Zacarias Moussaoui (charged in federal court); Yazid Sufaat (wanted in the U.S.)	Binyam Mohamed, Abu Zubaydah; Ramzi Bin al-Shibh; Mohammed al Qahtani	Human Rights First, "Not Full and Fair," *Human Rights First Blog*, March 2, 2006; Brian Ross and Richard Esposito, "CIA's Harsh Interrogation Techniques Described," *ABC News*, November 18, 2005; Douglas Jehl and Eric Lichtblau "Shift on Suspect is Linked to Role of Qaeda Figures," *New York Times*, November 24, 2005; Deborah Sontag, "In Padilla Wiretaps, Murky View of 'Jihad' Case," *New York Times*, January 4, 2007; "New Intelligence Report on New Generation of Terrorists; Clinton Defends Efforts to Get Bin Laden; Venezuela's Foreign Minister Angry at Airport Detention" CNN Transcript, September 24, 2006; Substitution for the Testimony of Khalid Sheikh Mohammed, Defendant's Exhibit 941, *U.S. v. Moussaoui*, C.R. No. 01-455-A; CIA Director Michael Hayden, Senate (Select) Intelligence Committee, Current and Projected National Security Threats, 110th Cong., 2ⁿ Sess., 2008; President George W. Bush, "President Discusses Creation of Military Commissions to Try Suspected Terrorists," White House news release, September 6, 2006; Office of the Assistant Secretary of Defense (Public Affairs), "Guantanamo Provides Valuable Intelligence Information," Department of Defense news release, June 12, 2005.
Khandan Kadir, No. 831	Detainee alleges he was forced to stand for 24 hours at a time for 20 days in a row, he had blood coming out of his body and nose due to torture, he was not fed for 2 days, he was made to stand in the dark for 15 days, and he was subjected to sensory deprivatiom.	Himself		CSRT Set 24, p. 1798-1820; ARB Set 9, p. 21017-21037.
Mahrar Rafat Al Quwari, No. 519	Detainee alleges he was "tortured" by the Northern Alliance for one month in a Kabul prison.	Himself		CSRT Set 31, p. 2145-2152.
Majid Ahmad, No. 041	Detainee alleges that interrogators stepped on his Koran and that prisoners are mocked during prayer.	Himself		Carol Rosenberg, "Captives Allege Religious Abuse" *Miami Herald*, March 6, 2005; Unclassified Summary of Evidence for CSRT, http://www.dod.mil/pubs/foi/detainees/csrt_arb/000001-000100.pdf#47.

Name of Detainee	Confirmed Abuse and Allegations of Abuse	Who Detainee Implicated or May Have Implicated	Who Implicated Detainee or May Have Implicated Detainee	Source of Information
Majid Khan (aka Yusif), HVD, No. 10020	The Bush administration has confirmed the use of "alternative" interrogation techniques on the detainee while in secret CIA custody. At his CSRT hearing, the detainee submitted a twelve-page "torture report" alleging abuse by the DoD and FBI (redacted in his CSRT transcript). Detainee (through reports from his brother, who was initially detained with him) alleges that, while in a Pakistani detention center, Americans tortured him for eight hours at a time, tied him in stress positions, beat him, deprived him of sleep, and kept him in the dark in a small mosquito-filled cell. Detainee also alleges that he has been subjected to "mental torture" and religious abuse at Guantánamo.	Himself; Mohd Farik bin Amin	Khalid Sheikh Mohammed; Iyman Faris (charged in federal court)	CSRT Set 10, p. 1089-1107; Michael Melia, "Attorneys Say Terror Suspect Tortured," *ABC News*, December 9. 2007; President George W. Bush, "President Discusses Creation of Military Commissions to Try Suspected Terrorists," White House news release, September 6, 2006; Adam Zagorin, "New Charges of Gitmo Torture," *Time*, February 6, 2008; President George W. Bush, "President Discusses Creation of Military Commissions to Try Suspected Terrorists," White House news release, September 6, 2006.
Mohamedou Ould Slahi (aka Abu Masab), No. 760	Detainee alleges that, while incarcerated in Mauritania, US agents hit him and threatened him with torture. Detainee alleges that he was released and then turned over to Jordan for eight months, where Jordanian interrogators hit him, slammed him against a concrete wall, and tortured and threatened him. Following his transfer to Bagram, detainee alleges he was grabbed with chains and dragged over concrete stairs. Detainee alleges that, at Guantánamo, he was sexually harassed, beaten, given medications that caused extended unconsciousness, and exposed to temperature extremes. The Schmidt-Furlow report confirmed that the detainee was subjected to extreme temperatures, threatened with death and disappearance and that his family was threatened.	Himself	Ramzi bin al-Shibh	CSRT Set 41, p. 2684-2694; ARB 8, p. 20934-20966; Lt. Gen. Mark Schmidt and Brig. Gen. John Furlow, Final Report, Investigation into FBI Allegations of Detainee Abuse at Guantánamo Bay, Cuba Detention Facility, (Department of Defense, June 9, 2005); Amnesty International Report, "USA: Rendition - torture - trial?: The case of Guantánamo detainee Mohamedou Ould Slahi," September 20, 2006; Human Rights Watch, "Double Jeopardy: CIA Renditions to Jordan," April 2008.
Mohammed Ahmed Said Haidel, No. 498	Detainee alleges that, while in a Kandahar prison, interrogators beat him with his hands tied behind his back until his head started bleeding.	Himself		CSRT Set 31, p. 2153-2155.

Name of Detainee	Confirmed Abuse and Allegations of Abuse	Who Detainee Implicated or May Have Implicated	Who Implicated Detainee or May Have Implicated Detainee	Source of Information
*Mohammed al-Qahtani, No. 063	Detainee alleges he was sleep deprived, subjected to loud music and white noise, exposed to extreme temperatures, beaten, subjected to forced nudity, sexually and religiously humiliated, forced to pray to Osama bin Laden, subjected to stress positions, subjected to loud music, subjected to "invasion of space by a female," leashed, not allowed to use the bathroom, subjected to 20-hour interrogations for months at a time, kept in severe isolation, threatened with dogs, had threats made against his family, subjected to stress positions, and threatened with transfer to countries that torture. The accidental disclosure of al-Qahtani's interrogation log confirmed many of these allegations. The Schmidt-Furlow report further confirmed that al-Qahtani was threatened with snarling dogs, forced to wear underwear on his head and led by a leash attached to his chains.	Himself; Abdulmalik Abdulwahhab Al-Rahabi; Farooq Ali Ahmed; Khalid Sheikh Mohammed; Othman Abdulraheem Mohammad; several other unnamed bodyguards of Osama bin Laden, some of whom remain at Guantánamo; Jose Padilla (charged in federal court); Richard Reid (charged in federal court; Adnan El Shukrijumah (wanted in the U.S.)	Khalid Sheikh Mohammed	Adam Zagorin and Michael Duffy, "Inside the Interrogation of Detainee 063," *Time*, June 12, 2005; Editorial, "A General's Dishonor," *Washington Post*, January 15, 2006; Lt. Gen. Mark Schmidt and Brig. Gen. John Furlow, Final Report, Investigation into FBI Allegations of Detainee Abuse at Guantánamo Bay, Cuba Detention Facility, (Department of Defense, June 9, 2005); Office of the Assistant Secretary of Defense (Public Affairs), "Guantanamo Provides Valuable Intelligence Information," Department of Defense news release, June 12, 2005; Adam Zagorin, "Exclusive: '20th Hijacker' Claims That Torture Made Him Lie," *Time*, February 3, 2006; ARB p. 2022-2033, http://humanrights.ucdavis.edu/projects/the-guantanamo-testimonials-project/testimonies/testimonies-of-the-defense-department/arb2s/arb2_063_2022-2033i.pdf; Letter from Marc D. Falkoff to Administrative Review Board, "Re: ARB Hearing for Abd al Malik Abd al Wahab, ISN 037," April 30, 2005 (on file with Human Rights First); Corine Hegland, "Guantanamo's Grip," *National Journal*, February 3, 2006; Letter from Marc D. Falkoff to Administrative Review Board, "Re: ARB Hearing for Faruq Ali Ahmed, ISN 032," February 5, 2005 (on file with Human Rights First); Letter from Marc D. Falkoff to Administrative Review Board, "Re: ARB Hearing for Uthman Abdul Rahim Mohammed Uthman," June 1, 2005 (on file with Human Rights First); Substitution for the Testimony of Khalid Sheikh Mohammed, Defendant's Exhibit 941, *U.S. v. Moussaoui*, C.R. No. 01-455-A.
Mohammed Bawazir, No. 440	Detainee alleges he was tortured.	Himself		ARB Set 6, p. 20430-20444.
*Mohammad Jawad, ISN 900	Detainee alleges he was tortured and beaten by Afghani police.	Himself		William Glaberson, "U.S. Files Charges Against Detainee," *New York Times*, October 11, 2007; Andy Worthington, "The Afghani Teen Put to Trial at Guantanamo," *Counterpunch*, October 17, 2007; ARB Set 9, p. 21147-21157.
Mohammed Mustafa Sohail, No. 1008	Detainee alleges interrogators beat him, tortured him and threatened him with a gun to his mouth at a U.S. facility in Kabul.	Himself		CSRT Set 33, p. 2325-2335; ARB Set 10, p. 21587-21606.

Name of Detainee	Confirmed Abuse and Allegations of Abuse	Who Detainee Implicated or May Have Implicated	Who Implicated Detainee or May Have Implicated Detainee	Source of Information
Mohammed Nasir Yahya Khusruf, No. 509	Detainee alleges he was beaten at an underground prison in Kabul.			CSRT Set 48, p. 3259-3270; ARB Set 7, p. 20497-20508.
Mohammed Nazir Bin Lep (aka Lillie; Bashir Bin Lep), HVD, No. 10022	The Bush administration has confirmed the use of "alternative" interrogation techniques on the detainee while in secret CIA custody.			Brian Ross and Richard Esposito, "CIA's Harsh Interrogation Techniques Described," *ABC News*, November 18, 2005; President George W. Bush, "President Discusses Creation of Military Commissions to Try Suspected Terrorists," White House news release, September 6, 2006.
Mohammed Nechle (aka Sharfuldin), No. 10003	Detainee alleges he was bound by his hands and feet, made to go 36 hours without food, sleep or water, forbidden to use the bathroom for 3 days, and denied medical treatment. Detainee further alleges that, during his transfer to Guantánamo, he was given only apples to eat and that his hands were bound so tight that he now has numb wrists.			CSRT Set 7, p. 741-755.
Mohammed Sulaymon Barre, No. 567	Detainee alleges he was grabbed by the neck and thrown, exposed to extreme temperatures, denied food, and denied medical treatment for at least 15-20 days while at Bagram.			CSRT Set 52, p. 3702-3709.
Mohd Farik bin Amin; (aka Zubair, Zaid), HVD, No. 10021	The Bush administration has confirmed the use of "alternative" interrogation techniques on the detainee while in secret CIA custody.	Riduan bin Isomuddin	Khalid Sheikh Mohammed; Majid Khan	Brian Ross and Richard Esposito, "CIA's Harsh Interrogation Techniques Described," *ABC News*, November 18, 2005; President George W. Bush, "President Discusses Creation of Military Commissions to Try Suspected Terrorists," White House news release, September 6, 2006.
Muhammad Abd Al Nasir Muhammad Khantumani, No. 312	Detainee alleges that, while in a Pakistani prison with Americans present, he was subjected to harsh torture and beatings, resulting in a broken nose. Detainee further alleges that he was tortured, sleep deprived, beaten and denied bathroom access at a U.S. prison in Kandahar. At Guantánamo, detainee alleges he was threatened with electric shocks, physical harm, and death, tortured, sleep deprived, not allowed to use the bathroom, beaten, twice told his family was killed, and threatened with transfer to a country known to torture.			CSRT Set 51, p. 3557-3571.

Name of Detainee	Confirmed Abuse and Allegations of Abuse	Who Detainee Implicated or May Have Implicated	Who Implicated Detainee or May Have Implicated Detainee	Source of Information
Muktar Warafi, No. 117	Detainee alleges he was threatened with rape.	Himself		Carol D. Leonnig and Dana Priest, "Detainees Accuse Female Interrogators," *Washington Post*, February 10, 2005.
Musab Omar Ali Al Mudwani, No. 839	Detainee alleges that, while in prison in Afghanistan, he was kept underground and interrogated, sleep deprived, kept in darkness, and beaten by Afghan soldiers and Arab-Americans.	Himself		CSRT Set 8, p. 1001-1011; ARB Set 9, p. 21046-21058.
*** Mustafa Ahmed al-Hawsawi** (aka Hashim Abd al Rahman; Zahir; Ayyub; Muhammed Andan), HVD, No. 10011	The Bush administration has confirmed the use of "alternative" interrogation techniques on the detainee while in secret CIA custody.	Himself	Khalid Sheikh Mohammed	President George W. Bush, "President Discusses Creation of Military Commissions to Try Suspected Terrorists," White House news release, September 6, 2006. Substitution for the Testimony of Mustafa Ahmed al-Hawsawi, Defendant's Exhibit 943, *U.S. v. Moussaoui*, C.R. No. 01-455-A; Substitution for the Testimony of Khalid Sheikh Mohammed, Defendant's Exhibit 941, *U.S. v. Moussaoui*, C.R. No. 01-455-A.
Mustafa Ait Idr, No. 10004	Detainee alleges he was inhumanely moved to Guantánamo Bay with a mask over his face and he could not feel his leg for four of five months after his arrival. Detainee further alleges that, after his arrival, he was verbally and physically abused, held under water in a toilet with a hose in his mouth to make him believe he was drowning, tear gassed, kept in isolation for two months, not allowed to pray, exposed to extreme temperatures, had his head banged into a steel bunk, had his finger broken, sprayed in the face with a chemical irritant and pinned on the floor while interrogators jumped on his head, resulting in a stroke and a paralyzed face.			CSRT Set 53, p. 3912-3935; ARB Set 12, p. 22218-22244; Charlie Savage, "Guantánamo Detainee is Alleging he was Brutalized," *Boston Globe*, April 13, 2005; Neil A. Lewis, "Guantánamo Detainees Suit Says Prison Guards Beat Him," *New York Times*, April 14, 2005; The New York Center for Constitutional Rights (CCR), "Report on Torture, Cruel, Inhuman, and Degrading Treatment of Prisoners at Guantánamo Bay, Cuba," July 2006.

Name of Detainee	Confirmed Abuse and Allegations of Abuse	Who Detainee Implicated or May Have Implicated	Who Implicated Detainee or May Have Implicated Detainee	Source of Information
Mustafa Ibrahim Mustafa Al Hassan, No. 719	Detainee alleges that, while at Bagram, he was tortured, beaten, given electric shocks and forced to walk on sharp objects.	Himself	Detainee alleges that interrogators told him that people he was detained with had implicated him. Detainee alleges that the people must have lied about him because they had been tortured.	CSRT Set 42, p. 2780-2789.
*Omar Ahmed Khadr, No. 766	Detainee alleges that, while held in Bagram, he was threatened with barking dogs, had water thrown on him, forced to carry heavy buckets of water, made to pick up trash, forced to urinate on himself, put in stress positions, and threatened with rape. In preparation for his transfer from Bagram to Guantanamo, detainee alleges he was deprived of food for two nights and one day, had his head and beard shaved, and subjected to sensory deprivation. En route to Guantanamo, detainee alleges he was shackled to the floor and kicked in the leg. At Guantanamo, detainee alleges he was repeatedly pushed into the wall until he passed out, interrogators pulled his hair and spit in his face, he was forced to spend one month in isolation in a room that felt "like a refrigerator," had his hands tied to the door frame and made to dangle for hours, subjected to stress positions, threatened with transfer to countries known to torture, repeatedly lifted in the air and dropped to the floor, used as a "human mop," repeatedly kneed in the thighs, and grabbed by pressure points.	Himself		Affidavit of Omar Ahmed Khadr, 2/22/08, http://media.miamiherald.com/smedia/2008/03/18/14/Redacted_Khadr_Affidavit_22_Feb_2008.source.prod_affiliate.56.pdf; Human Rights First, "Military Commission Hearing Preview," *Human Rights First Blog*, January 10, 2006; The New York Center for Constitutional Rights (CCR), "Report on Torture, Cruel, Inhuman, and Degrading Treatment of Prisoners at Guantánamo Bay, Cuba," July 2006; *O.K. v. Bush*, 377 F. Supp. 2d 102, 103 (D.D.C. 2005); Unclassified Summary of Evidence for CSRT, http://www.dod.mil/pubs/foi/detainees/csrt_arb/000600-000699.pdf#7.

Name of Detainee	Confirmed Abuse and Allegations of Abuse	Who Detainee Implicated or May Have Implicated	Who Implicated Detainee or May Have Implicated Detainee	Source of Information
Omar Hamzayavich Abdulayev, No. 257	Detainee alleges he was beaten and tortured by Pakistani intelligence officials for one month.	Himself		CSRT Set 20, p. 1608-1613.
Othman Abdulraheem Mohammad (aka Mohammed Abdul Rahim Uthman), No. 027	Detainee alleges he was subjected to fluorescent light for 24 hours a day for 3 years, resulting in eye pain and dizziness.	Himself	Mohammed al-Qahtani	Letter from Marc D. Falkoff to Administrative Review Board, "Re: ARB Hearing for Uthman Abdul Rahim Mohammed Uthman," June 1, 2005 (on file with Human Rights First); The New York Center for Constitutional Rights (CCR), "Report on Torture, Cruel, Inhuman, and Degrading Treatment of Prisoners at Guantánamo Bay, Cuba," July 2006.
Rafiq bin Bashir bin Jalud Al Hami, No. 892	Detainee alleges that, while held in Afghanistan, Americans tortured him, threatened him, left him out all night in the cold, and no shoes, in the darkness and in the cold, subjected him to loud music for two months, prevented him from praying, and did not permit him to fast during Ramadan.	Himself		CSRT Set 34, p. 2445-2447; ARB Set 3, p. 913-927.
*Ramzi Bin al-Shibh (aka Abu Ubaydah; Umar Muhammad Abduallah Ba Amar), HVD, No. 10013	The Bush administration has confirmed the use of "alternative" interrogation techniques on the detainee while in secret CIA custody. A former detainee who was held in the cell next to al-Shibh during his detention in Jordan alleges that Jordanian officials subjected al-Shibh to electric shocks, sleep deprivation, forced nudity, and made him sit on sticks and bottles.	Khalid Sheikh Mohammed; Mohamedou Ould Slahi	Abu Zubaydah; Khalid Sheikh Mohammed	"New Intelligence Report on New Generation of Terrorists; Clinton Defends Efforts to Get Bin Laden; Venezuela's Foreign Minister Angry at Airport Detention," CNN Transcript, September 24, 2006; President George W. Bush, "President Discusses Creation of Military Commissions to Try Suspected Terrorists," White House news release, September 6, 2006; Mohamedou Ould Slahi ARB Set 8, p. 20934-20966; Amnesty International Report, "USA: Rendition - torture - trial?: The case of Guantánamo detainee Mohamedou Ould Slahi," September 20, 2006; Substitution for the Testimony of Khalid Sheikh Mohammed, Defendant's Exhibit 941, *U.S. v. Moussaoui*, C.R. No. 01-455-A; Human Rights Watch, "Double Jeopardy: CIA Renditions to Jordan," April 2008.
Riduan bin Isomuddin (aka Hambali; Encep Nurjaman), HVD, No. 10019	The Bush administration has confirmed the use of "alternative" interrogation techniques on the detainee while in secret CIA custody.	Himself	Mohd Farik bin Amin; Khalid Sheikh Mohammed	Substitution for the Testimony of Riduan Isamuddin ("Hambali"), Defendant's Exhibit 946, *U.S. v. Moussaoui*, C.R. No. 01-455-A; President George W. Bush, "President Discusses Creation of Military Commissions to Try Suspected Terrorists," White House news release, September 6, 2006.
Sada Jan, No. 1035	Detainee alleges that Americans hit him and badly beat him and that he was denied medical care at Guantánamo.	Himself		CSRT Set 32, p. 2266-2278; ARB Set 11, p. 21683-21698.

Name of Detainee	Confirmed Abuse and Allegations of Abuse	Who Detainee Implicated or May Have Implicated	Who Implicated Detainee or May Have Implicated Detainee	Source of Information
Saifullah Paracha, No. 1094	Detainee alleges he was cuffed at his legs and hands, masked, thrown face down on the floor, and kept in isolation.			CSRT Set 10, p. 1089-1107.
*Salim Ahmed Hamdan, No. 149	Detainee alleges he was beaten, subjected to stress positions, threatened with death and torture, dressed in light overalls in sub-freezing temperatures, kept in severe isolation, and made to sit motionless for days.	Himself		Human Rights First, "Facing Mr. Hamdan," *Human Rights First Blog*, November 8, 2004; Unclassified Summary of Evidence for CSRT, http://www.dod.mil/pubs/foi/detainees/csrt_arb/000101-000200.pdf#48; Mark Tran, "Profile: Salim Ahmed Hamdan," *Guardian (UK)*, June 5, 2007.
Sami al-Hajj, No. 345	Detainee alleges he was kept in a freezing cage, intimidated with dogs, kept in stress positions, threatened with rape, had his hair plucked, beaten, pepper-sprayed, held in isolation, sleep deprived, sexually and racially abused, denied medical care, sensory deprived, deprived of food, subjected to religious abuse, and had threats made against his family.			Amnesty International USA, "Who are the Guantanamo Detainees?, Case Sheet 16," January 11, 2006; "The Guantanamo Detainee (al-Hajj)," *Al Jazeera English*, October 31, 2006; Reporters Without Borders, "Camp Bucca and Guantanamo Bay, Where the United States Imprisons Journalists," February 2006; Roshan Muhammed Salih, "Aljazeera Guantanamo Inmate 'Abused,'" *Al Jazeera English*, June 23, 2005.
Sanad Ali Yislam Al-Kazimi, No. 1453	Detainee alleges that, at the Dark Prison in Afghanistan, he was suspended by his arms for long periods, causing his legs to swell, and that while hanging he was beaten with electric cables.	Himself		Jane Mayer, "The Black Sites: A rare look inside the C.I.A.'s secret interrogation program," *New Yorker*, August 13, 2007; CSRT Set 34, p. 2451-2453.
Shakhrukh Hamiduva, No. 022	Detainee alleges he was tortured, sleep deprived, and denied medical care.	Himself		CSRT Set 47, p. 3199-3209.
Sufyian Barhoumi, No. 694	Detainee alleges he walked for an hour and a half with chains on, resulting in a bandaged leg, and he was offered surgery but refused.	Himself		CSRT Set 12, p. 1200-1214.

Name of Detainee	Confirmed Abuse and Allegations of Abuse	Who Detainee Implicated or May Have Implicated	Who Implicated Detainee or May Have Implicated Detainee	Source of Information
Sulaiman Awath Sulaiman Bin Ageel Al Nahdi, No. 511	Detainee alleges he was tortured in a Kabul prison.	Himself		CSRT Set 18, p. 1522.
*Walid Bin Attash (aka Khallad Bin Attash; Silver), HVD, No. 10014	The Bush administration has confirmed the use of "alternative" interrogation techniques on the detainee while in secret CIA custody.	Zacarias Moussaoui (charged in federal court)	Khalid Sheikh Mohammed	Substitution for the Testimony of Walid Muhammad Salih Bin Attash ("Khallad"), Defendant's Exhibit 945, *U.S. v. Moussaoui*, C.R. No. 01-455-A; Substitution for the Testimony of Khalid Sheikh Mohammed, Defendant's Exhibit 941, *U.S. v. Moussaoui*, C.R. No. 01-455-A President George W. Bush, "President Discusses Creation of Military Commissions to Try Suspected Terrorists," White House news release, September 6, 2006.
Yasin Qasem Muhammad Ismail, No. 522	Detainee alleges he was tortured, beaten, tied with his foot to his back and thrown on his face, kicked and stomped on, thrown in the air and allowed to fall, left under air conditioning for 18 hours, sleep deprived, and sexually abused.	Himself		CSRT Set 53, p. 3953-3958; ARB Set 1, p. 959-960; The New York Center for Constitutional Rights (CCR), "Report on Torture, Cruel, Inhuman, and Degrading Treatment of Prisoners at Guantánamo Bay, Cuba," July 2006; Richard A. Serrano, "Guantanamo Bay Justice," *Los Angeles Times*, November 7, 2004; Carol D. Leonnig and Dana Priest, "Detainees Accuse Female Interrogators," *Washington Post*, February 10, 2005.

C. Enhanced Interrogation Techniques

Descriptions of enhanced interrogation techniques used by CIA and military interrogators and their legal consequences

Table starts next page.

C. Enhanced Interrogation Techniques

Descriptions of enhanced interrogation techniques and their legal consequences

Unless otherwise cited, the information in this chart is derived from: Human Rights First and Physicians for Human Rights, *Leave No Marks: Enhanced Interrogation Techniques and the Risk of Criminality* (New York: Human Rights First and Physicians for Human Rights, August 2007), http://www.humanrightsfirst.info/pdf/07801-etn-leave-no-marks.pdf.

Note: These techniques are almost always used in combination, severely magnifying the effects.

Enhanced Interrogation Technique	Physical and Psychological Harm	U.S. Supreme Court Decisions & War Crimes Tribunals	State Department Classifications
Stress Positions Forced painful physical positions maintained for prolonged periods, including forced standing, awkward sitting or kneeling, and suspension of the body from chains or other implements.	1. Long-term or permanent nerve, joint, and circulatory injuries and lesions, and 2. Immobility from prolonged standing, which can result in: a. musculoskeletal foot and back pain, b. fatal blood clots, c. pulmonary embolism if/when prolonged standing results in fainting, causing blunt trauma force from head injuries and fractures, and d. damaged peripheral nerves, decreasing both motor sensation and the ability to feel temperature or vibrations.	In *Hope v. Pelzer*, 536 U.S. 730, 741 (2002), the Supreme Court held that the use of certain stress positions violates the Eight Amendment and offends contemporary concepts of decency. The Supreme Court has also held that the Due Process Clause affords prisoners freedom from unnecessary bodily restraint. *See Youngberg v. Romeo*, 457 U.S. 307, 316 (1982). *See also Davis v. Rennie*, 264 F.3d 86 (1st Cit. 1981). This Supreme Court precedent suggests that the use of stress positions in interrogations likely violateshe Detainee Treatment Act.	The State Department has criticized Burma, Israel, and North Korea for the use of forced painful positions during interrogations as examples of abuse, torture, or cruel, inhuman, or degrading treatment. The State Department has also condemned the use of suspension and hanging by limbs in Egypt, Indonesia, Iran, Iraq, Jordan, Libya, North Korea, Pakistan, Saudi Arabia, Tunisia, and Turkey. See Human Rights Watch, "Examples of Torture or other Cruel, Inhuman, or Degrading Treatment Condemned in the U.S. State Department's 2003 Country Reports on Human Rights Practices," (hereafter "Examples of Torture"), http://www.hrw.org/campaigns/torture/methods/stress_duress.htm.

Enhanced Interrogation Technique	Physical and Psychological Harm	U.S. Supreme Court Decisions & War Crimes Tribunals	State Department Classifications
Beating Blows of forceful physical contact delivered in a variety of ways, including through instruments. Often given benign names, such as "attention slap" or "belly slap."	1. Blunt trauma and massive bruising from ruptured blood vessels, 2. Long-term muscle and joint pain, 3. Symptoms of post-traumatic stress disorder, 4. Damage to underlying body muscle tissue, which can enter the circulation system and lead to a life-threatening kidney condition, 5. Open hand slapping, which diffuses blunt trauma force over a larger area, and can case neck injuries, soft tissue injuries, lacerations, and fractures of vulnerable facial bones and features.	The Supreme Court has recognized that the right to bodily integrity and the right to be free from the intentional infliction of unnecessary pain are two of the most fundamental rights protected by the Fifth and Fourteenth Amendments. See *Albright v. Oliver*, 510 U.S. 266, 272 (1994); *Washington v. Glucksberg*, 521 U.S. 702, 719 (1977); *Ingraham v. Wright*, 430 U.S. 651, 670 (1977). See also *Ware v. Reed*, 709 F.2d 347, 351 (5th Cir. 1983) (holding that "no physical force is constitutionally permissible" during interrogation). Supreme Court precedent suggests that beating a prisoner likely violates the Detainee Treatment Act. During the International Military Tribunals in the Far East following WWII, Japanese interrogators were prosecuted for the beatings of U.S. POWs. Following the Gulf War, the United States filed a U.N. report stating that Iraqis had committed war crimes for slapping U.S. POWs.	Despite the use of beatings in U.S. interrogations, the State Department has condemned at least 16 countries for using beatings as an interrogation technique, citing it as a type of abuse or example of torture or cruel, inhuman, or degrading treatment. Countries include Brazil, Burma, China, Egypt, Eritrea, Indonesia, Iran, Iraq, Libya, North Korea, Pakistan, Saudi Arabia, Tunisia, Turkey, Uzbekistan, and Zimbabwe. The State Department has also criticized Turkey for the use of slapping during interrogations. See Human Rights Watch, "Examples of Torture."

Enhanced Interrogation Technique	Physical and Psychological Harm	U.S. Supreme Court Decisions & War Crimes Tribunals	State Department Classifications
Temperature Manipulation Exposure to extreme heat or to extreme cold for prolonged periods.	1. Hypothermia, 2. Prolonged neurological consequences of hypothermia include slowed mental functioning, diminished reflexes, and flaccid muscle tone, 3. Slowed gastrointestinal function, 4. Decreased resistance to infection, 5. Slowed heart function, triggering arrhythmias (irregular heartbeats), ventricular fibrillation, and cardiac arrest, 6. Amnesia and other cognitive failure, 7. Drops below 86°F can result in loss of consciousness, major organ failure, and death, and 8. Increased body temperatures above 104°F can result in heat stroke, causing delirium, convulsions, comas and possibly death.	The Supreme Court has held that the Fifth and Eighth Amendments require the government to provide clothing and shelter to detainees as a matter of due process. *See Deshaney v. Washington*, 489 U.S. 189, 199-200 (1989). Additionally, the Court has held that indifference to these basic needs violates prisoners' rights under the Fifth, Eighth, and Fourteenth Amendments. *See id.* This precedent suggests that the use of extreme temperatures may violate the Detainee Treatment Act. During the Korean War, Chinese interrogators subjected U.S. troops to extreme temperatures to extract false confessions.	In 2005, the State Department criticized Syria and Turkey for practicing torture by exposing prisoners to cold temperatures and dousing victims in freezing cold water while beating them in extremely cold rooms. In 2006, the State Department categorized these techniques as "forms of torture and abuse."
Waterboarding Mock drowning by strapping down and immobilizing the body while water is poured over the face, which is usually wrapped in tight fabric.	1. Severe physical responses, resulting in hypoxia (oxygen depletion), neurological damage; near asphyxiation, triggering bleeding into the skin, nose and ear bleeding; facial congestion; mouth infections, and acute or chronic respiratory problems; and fatal aspiration pneumonia if liquid enters the lungs, 2. Severe and unavoidable physiological responses, resulting in tachyradia (rapid heart beat); hyperventilation, and breathlessness, which can itself provoke cardiac ischemia (obstruction of blood flow to the heart) or arrhythmia; and long-term head and back pain, and 3. Severe psychological harm, including profound sensory disruption, respiratory panic attacks, strong symptoms of depression, long-term trauma, and prolonged post-traumatic stress disorder.	The Supreme Court's recognition of the Fifth and Fourteenth Amendment rights to bodily integrity and freedom from intentional infliction of unnecessary pain suggests that the physical sensation of suffocation resulting from waterboarding violates the Detainee Treatment Act. *See Albright*, 510 U.S. at 272. In addition, U.S. federal courts have characterized waterboarding as torture. *See, e.g., Hilao v. Marco*, 103 F.3d 789, 790 (9th Cir. 1996). In 1947, a Japanese military official was convicted of a war crime for waterboarding an American civilian. The United States sentenced him to fifteen years of hard labor.	In March 2007, the State Department criticized Sri Lanka for using the torture technique of "near-drowning." From 1996-2004, the State Department repeatedly criticized Tunisia of practicing torture by submerging victims' heads in water. In 2003, the State Department criticized Brazil and Tunisia for engaging in waterbording and Turkey for engaging in human rights abuses by dripping water on victims' heads. *See* Human Rights Watch, "Examples of Torture."

Enhanced Interrogation Technique	Physical and Psychological Harm	U.S. Supreme Court Decisions & War Crimes Tribunals	State Department Classifications
Threats of Harm to Person, Family or Friends Threats of harm such as dismemberment, castration, or mock execution for failure to cooperate with interrogators.	1. Extreme fear and loss of control strongly associated with post-traumatic stress disorder and severe depression, 2. Flashbacks, intrusive memories, and nightmares of near-death interrogations, and 3. Intense anxiety leading to self harm and suicidal behavior, especially true of victims who experience mock executions and acquire a sense of complete uncertainty and fear by reliving the last moments before their anticipated death.	Courts have found that verbal threats of the use of deadly force can violate the Fifth and Fourteenth Amendments. See, e.g., *Hawkins v. Holloway*, 316 F.3d 777, 787 (8th Cir. 2003). During the first Gulf War, the United States accused Iraq of war crimes for conducting mock executions, pointing pistols at prisoners' heads, dry-firing pistols into prisoners' mouths, and threatening U.S. POWs with dismemberment or castration during interrogations.	Since at least 2002, the State Department has classified the practice of threatening prisoners used by Brazil, Egypt, and Tunisia as a form of torture or cruel, inhuman, or degrading treatment. In 2003, the State Department criticized the use of threats, especially of sexual abuse, used by Brazil, Egypt, Iraq, Israel, Tunisia, and Turkey. See Human Rights Watch, "Examples of Torture."
Sleep Deprivation Denial of sleep for extended periods to destroy psychological resistance to interrogation. Usually includes the use of stress positions and sensory overload.	1. Hypertension, cardiovascular disease, altered glucose tolerance, insulin resistance, impaired immune function, and increased risk of infectious diseases, 2. Chronic pain syndromes linked to disrupted sleep patterns, 3. Significant cognitive impairment, including deficiencies in memory, learning, logical reasoning, complex verbal reasoning, and decision-making, and 4. Decreased psychomotor performance, mood alterations, psychiatric disorders, major depression, and risk of suicidal thoughts.	The Supreme Court has held that a confession obtained after 36 hours of sleep deprivation violates a prisoner's right to due process. See *Ashcraft v. Tennessee*, 322 U.S. 143, 154 (1944). Justice Black noted that, since at least 1500, "deprivation of sleep is the most effective torture and certain to produce any confession desired." See *id.* at n.6.	The State Department has condemned the use of sleep deprivation by Indonesia, Iran, Jordan, Libya, Saudi Arabia, and Turkey as a form of torture or cruel, inhuman, or degrading treatment. In 2003, the State Department criticized Indonesia, Iran, Israel, Jordan, Libya, Saudi Arabia, and Turkey for their use of sleep deprivation as a human rights abuse. See Human Rights Watch, "Examples of Torture."
Sensory Bombardment Noise and Light Jarring the senses for extended periods to cause physiological distress and encourage disorientation and withdrawal from reality. Overexposure to bright lights, flashing strobe lights, and blaring or loud music.	1. Release of stress hormones that raise the risk of heart disease or heart attack by certain noises, interpreted as danger signals, 2. Hearing loss or chronic tinnitus (ringing in the ears) from loud music, 3. Strobe lights can cause increased heart rate and blood pressure, and serious symptoms common of headlight glare, including potentially fatal electrical rhythmic disturbances of the heart, and 4. Sleep deprivation and its subsequent impairments.	The Supreme Court has held that the use of a confession obtained by shining a bright light in the eyes of a suspect during a 36 hour interrogation violated due process. See *Ashcraft*, 322 U.S. 143.	The State Department has criticized Burma for the use of bright lights during long interrogations, and condemned Turkey's use of sensory bombardment through loud music as a form of torture from 1992-2002.

Enhanced Interrogation Technique	Physical and Psychological Harm	U.S. Supreme Court Decisions & War Crimes Tribunals	State Department Classifications
Violent Shaking Forceful and violent shaking of the upper torso in a back-and-forth motion so that the head and neck dangle and vacillate rapidly. Sometimes referred to as the "attention grab."	1. Serious brain damage, 2. Permanent neurological deficiencies, 3. Intracranial pressure, 4. Death from resulting retinal hemorrhages, intracranial hemorrhages, and cerebral edema (the swelling of the brain), 5. "Shaken Baby Syndrome" (brain matter is fatally squeezed through the brainstem when swelling or bleeding reaches dangerous levels), 6. Recurring or chronic headaches, disorientation, and mental status changes, and 7. Neck trauma and cervical spine fracture, which can result in quadriplegia.	N/A	N/A
Sexual Humiliation Subjugation to sexually humiliating behavior or forced performance of sexually humiliating acts. Exploitation of cultural and religious stereotypes regarding sexual behavior to induce feelings of shame, guilt and worthlessness.	1. Post traumatic stress disorder, major depression, reliving of the humiliation through flashbacks and nightmares, and destruction of a sense of self-identity and self-autonomy, 2. Assault on cultural and religious taboos can result in: a. intense shame, guilt of self-degradation, fear, and social isolation, and b. constant worry and over-alertness, triggering asthma, ulcers, colitis, and hypertension, and 3. emasculation often targeted toward male victims, resulting in especially devastating effects.	The Supreme Court has repeatedly held that the Eighth and Fourteenth Amendments guarantee the right to human dignity. See *Trop v. Dulls*, 356 U.S. 86, 101 (1958). Supreme Court precedent strongly suggests that sexual humiliation as an interrogation technique violates the Detainee Treatment Act.	The State Department has continuously criticized governments such as Egypt and Turkey for engaging in torture by forcing detainees to strip in front of the opposite sex, threatening them with rape, and inflicting sexual touching or threats. In 2003, the State Department characterized the use of sexual assault and sexual abuse during interrogations by Egypt, Eritrea, Iraq, Libya, Pakistan, Tunisia, Turkey, and Uzbekistan as a form of torture or cruel, inhuman, or degrading treatment. The 2003 reports additionally condemned the use of threats, especially of sexual abuse, used by Brazil, Egypt, Iraq, Israel, Tunisia, and Turkey. See Human Rights Watch, "Examples of Torture."

Enhanced Interrogation Technique	Physical and Psychological Harm	U.S. Supreme Court Decisions & War Crimes Tribunals	State Department Classifications
Prolonged Isolation and Sensory Deprivation Prolonged Isolation: Denying contact with others, including other prisoners, for prolonged periods to foster a sense of utter helplessness. Sensory Deprivation: Obstructing use of the senses for prolonged periods to create a sense of dependency on the interrogator.	1. Complete dependency, inducing severe anxiety and hallucinations, 2. Prolonged isolation triggers: a. increased stress, abnormal neuroendocrine function, and changes in blood pressure and inflammatory stress responses, and b. symptoms of bewilderment, anger, depression, obsession, paranoia, hypersensitivity, low self-esteem, and suicidal behavior, and 3. Even short-term isolation can result in concentration difficulty, bodily discomfort, disorientation, inability to complete tasks, hallucination, and loss of motor coordination.	The Supreme Court has held that solitary confinement may be justified under certain circumstances for administrative and security reasons, but it is unlikely to be justified for purposes of interrogation. See *Sandin v. Conner*, 515 U.S. 472 (1995).	The State Department has continuously criticized Jordan's use of prolonged isolation as a form of torture. In 2003, the State Department also criticized China, Iraq, North Korea, Pakistan, and Tunisia for engaging in solitary confinement practices as a form of torture. See Human Rights Watch, "Examples of Torture."

Endnotes

[1] President George W. Bush, "President Discusses Creation of Military Commissions to Try Suspected Terrorists," White House Press Briefing, September 6, 2006, (emphasis added), http://www.whitehouse.gov/news/releases/2006/09/20060906-3.html.

[2] *Sanchez-Llamas. v. Oregon*, 126 S. Ct. 2669, 2681 (2006).

[3] Michael Hirsh, John Barry and Daniel Klaidman, "A Tortured Debate," *Newsweek*, June 21, 2004, http://www.newsweek.com/id/54093.

[4] Dan Eggen and Walter Pincus, "FBI, CIA Debate Significance of Terror Suspect," *Washington Post*, December 18, 2007, http://www.washingtonpost.com/wp-dyn/content/article/2007/12/17/AR2007121702151.html.

[5] "Because in the beginning, while, like I say, he was friendly—and he was willing to talk about philosophy, he was unwilling to give us any—any actionable intelligence." Former CIA agent John Kiriakou, interview by Brian Ross, "CIA—Abu Zubaydah," ABC News transcript, Tape #1, December 10, 2007, http://abcnews.go.com/images/Blotter/brianross_kiriakou_transcript1_blotter071210.pdf.

[6] 18 U.S.C. §§ 2340-2340A (2006).

[7] Memorandum from Assistant Attorney General Jay S. Bybee, Office of Legal Counsel, to Alberto R. Gonzales, Counsel to the President, "Standards of Conduct for Interrogation under 18 U.S.C. §§ 2340-2340A," August 1, 2002, http://www.humanrightsfirst.org/us_law/etn/gonzales/memos_dir/memo_20020801_JD_%20Gonz_.pdf (hereafter "Bybee memorandum"). The Bybee memorandum also served as the legal basis for another memorandum, authored by Assistant Attorney General John Yoo, which reportedly details the permissible interrogation methods. Memorandum from John C. Yoo, Deputy Assistant Attorney General, Office of Legal Counsel, to Alberto R. Gonzales, Counsel to the President, August 1, 2002, http://news.findlaw.com/wp/docs/doj/bybee80102ltr.html; Memorandum from Daniel Levin, Acting Assistant Attorney General, Office of Legal Counsel to William J. Haynes II, General Counsel of the Department of Defense, "Re: Memorandum for William J. Haynes II, General Counsel of the Department of Defense, from John Yoo, Deputy Assistant Attorney General, Office of Legal Counsel, Re: Military Interrogation of Alien Unlawful Combatants Held Outside the United States (March 14, 2003)," February 4, 2005, http://balkin.blogspot.com/Levin.Haynes.205.pdf.

[8] Memorandum from William E. Moschella, Assistant Attorney General, to Senator Patrick J. Leahy, "Obligations of the United States under Article 16 of the U.N. Convention Against Torture," April 4, 2005, (on file with Human Rights First); Memorandum from President George W. Bush to the Vice President, et al., "Humane Treatment of al Qaeda and Taliban Detainees," February 7, 2002, http://www.gwu.edu/~nsarchiv/NSAEBB/NSAEBB127/02.02.07.pdf (hereafter "President Bush, February 2002 Memorandum"), stating that the U.S. government considered the Geneva Conventions inapplicable to captured members of al-Qaeda, and failing to mention parallel U.S. treaty obligations under the U.N. Convention Against Torture and the International Covenant of Civil and Political Rights.

[9] John Kiriakou, interview by Brian Ross, Tape #1, (admitting that the CIA used "enhanced techniques," including the attention slap, waterboarding and sleep deprivation of 40 hours plus). In 2005, ABC News reported that the CIA's interrogation program consisted of six "enhanced interrogation techniques," describing them as follows: "(1) The Attention Grab: The interrogator forcefully grabs the shirt front of the prisoner and shakes him. (2) Attention Slap: An open-handed slap aimed at causing pain and triggering fear. (3) The Belly Slap: A hard open-handed slap to the stomach. The aim is to cause pain, but not internal injury. Doctors consulted advised against using a punch, which could cause lasting internal damage. (4) Long Time Standing: This technique is described as among the most effective. Prisoners are forced to stand, handcuffed and with their feet shackled to an eye bolt in the floor for more than 40 hours. Exhaustion and sleep deprivation are effective in yielding confessions. (5) The Cold Cell: The prisoner is left to stand naked in a cell kept near 50 degrees. Throughout the time in the cell the prisoner is doused with cold water. (6) Water Boarding: The prisoner is bound to an inclined board, feet raised and head slightly below the feet. Cellophane is wrapped over the prisoner's face and water is poured over him. Unavoidably, the gag reflex kicks in and a terrifying fear of drowning leads to almost instant pleas to bring the treatment to a halt." Brian Ross and Richard Esposito, "CIA's Harsh Interrogation Techniques Described," ABCNews.com, November 18, 2005, http://abcnews.go.com/WNT/Investigation/story?id=1322866. Additionally, relying on intelligence sources familiar with a secret CIA report, James Risen in 2006 reported that: "Prisoners have been forced into coffin-like boxes, forced into cells where they are alternately denied all light and put in brightly lit rooms and denied sleep for long periods. They are subjected to

long hours of extremely loud rap music—Eminem is one favorite—and they are forced to stand or squat in 'stress positions' for hours at a time." James Risen, *State of War: The Secret History of the CIA and the Bush Administration* (New York: Free Press, 2006), p. 32.

[10] Douglas Jehl, "Report Warned C.I.A. on Tactics In Interrogation," *New York Times*, November 9, 2005, http://www.nytimes.com/2005/11/09/politics/09detain.html; Dana Priest, "Covert CIA Program Withstands New Furor," *Washington Post*, December 30, 2005, http://www.washingtonpost.com/wp-dyn/content/article/2005/12/29/AR2005122901585.html.

[11] Memorandum from Daniel Levin, Acting Assistant Attorney General to James B. Comey, Deputy Attorney General, "Re: Legal Standards Applicable Under 18 U.S.C. §§ 2340-2340A," December 30, 2004, fn. 8, http://www.humanrightsfirst.org/us_law/etn/pdf/levin-memo-123004.pdf. Testifying before Congress in February 2008, Assistant Attorney General Steven Bradbury described the term "severe physical suffering," outlined in the December 2004 memorandum, as suffering that "has to take account of both the intensity of the discomfort or distress involved and the duration, and something can be quite distressing or uncomfortable even frightening—but if it doesn't involve severe physical pain and it doesn't last very long, it may not constitute severe physical suffering." Prepared Statement of Principal Deputy Assistant Attorney General Steven Bradbury, House Committee on the Judiciary Subcommittee on Constitution, Civil Rights and Civil Liberties, *Justice Department's Office of Legal Counsel*, 110th Cong., 2nd sess., 2008.

[12] Detainee Treatment Act of 2005, Pub. L. No. 109-148, §1003(a).

[13] *Hamdan v. Rumsfeld*, 126 S. Ct. 2749, 2793-98 (2006).

[14] David Ignatius, "A Way Out of Guantánamo Bay," *Washington Post*, July 7, 2006, http://www.washingtonpost.com/wp-dyn/content/article/2006/07/06/AR2006070601548.html.

[15] Executive Order no. 13440, "Interpretation of the Geneva Conventions Common Article 3 as Applied to a Program of Detention and Interrogation Operated by the Central Intelligence Agency, July 20, 2007," *Federal Register*, 72, no. 141, 40705-09 (July 24, 2007), http://a257.g.akamaitech.net/7/257/2422/01jan20071800/edocket.access.gpo.gov/2007/pdf/07-3656.pdf. *See also* CIA Director General Michael V. Hayden, "Statement to Employees by Director of the Central Intelligence Agency, General Michael V. Hayden on the Executive Order on Detentions and Interrogations," CIA Press Statement, July 20, 2007, https://www.cia.gov/news-information/press-releases-statements/press-release-archive-2007/statement-on-executive-order.html; Greg Miller, "Bush Signs New CIA Interrogation Rules," *Los Angeles Times*, July 21, 2007.

[16] "No one has ever claimed that the Army Field Manual exhausts all the lawful interrogation techniques that the American republic can use to defend itself," said Hayden. CIA Director General Michael Hayden, interview by Charlie Rose, "Transcript: Charlie Rose interviews Michael Hayden," *International Herald Tribune (October 22, 2007)*, October 23, 2007, http://www.iht.com/articles/2007/10/23/america/23hayden.php?page=1. The new Army Field Manual, issued September 6, 2006 specifically prohibits the general application of physical pain. Department of the Army, *Field Manual No. 2-22.3: Human Intelligence Collector Operations* (Washington, DC: Department of the Army, September 6, 2006), secs. 5.73-76 (hereafter "*Army Field Manual 2-22.3*").

[17] Attorney General Michael Mukasey, Senate Committee on the Judiciary, *Oversight of the U.S. Department of Justice*, 110th Cong., 2nd sess., 2008.

[18] Staff Judge Advocate Diane Beaver's legal analysis accompanied the request. According to her reading, the requested techniques, including stress positions, isolation and use of phobias, did not violate federal law. Memorandum from Diane E. Beaver, Staff Judge Advocate, Department of Defense, Joint Task Force 170, to General James T. Hill, Commander, Joint Task Force 170, "Re: Legal Brief on Proposed Counter-Resistance Strategies," October 11, 2002; Memorandum by Jerald Phifer, Director J2, Department of Defense, Joint Task Force 170, to General James T. Hill, Commander, Joint Task Force 170, "Re: Request for Approval of Counter-Resistance Strategies," October 11, 2002; Memorandum by Diane E. Beaver, Staff Judge Advocate, Department of Defense, Joint Task Force 170, to General James T. Hill, Commander, Joint Task Force 170, "Re: Legal Review of Aggressive Interrogation Techniques," October 11, 2002. Memoranda available in *The Torture Papers: The Road to Abu Ghraib*, eds. Karen J. Greenberg and Joshua L. Dratel (New York: Cambridge University Press, 2005), pp. 229-235, 227-228, 226.

[19] Memorandum from William J. Haynes II, General Counsel, Department of Defense, to Donald Rumsfeld, Secretary of Defense, "Counter-Resistance Techniques," November 27, 2002; Memorandum from Jerald Phifer, to General James T. Hill, "Re: Request for Approval of Counter-Resistance Strategies," October 11, 2002. Memoranda available in *The Torture Papers*, pp. 236-237, 227-228.

[20] Memorandum from Alberto J. Mora, Navy General Counsel, to Navy Inspector General, "Re: Statement for the Record: Office of General Counsel Involvement in Interrogation Issues," July 7, 2004, p.14, http://www.aclu.org/safefree/torture/29228res20040707.html#attach (hereafter "Mora memo"); Bill Dedman, "Battle Over Tactics Raged at Gitmo" MSNBC.com, October 23, 2006, http://www.msnbc.msn.com/id/15361458/; FBI e-mail from [redacted] to Gary Bald, Frankie Battle, and Arthur Cummings, "Fwd: Impersonating FBI at GTMO," December 5, 2003, http://www.aclu.org/torturefoia/released/FBI.121504.3977.pdf; Jane Mayer, "Outsourcing Torture," *New Yorker*, February 14, 2005, http://www.newyorker.com/archive/2005/02/14/050214fa_fact6.

[21] Memorandum from Donald Rumsfeld, Secretary of Defense, to Commander USSOUTHCOM, "Counter-Resistance Techniques (U)," January 15, 2003, http://www.washingtonpost.com/wp-srv/nation/documents/011503rumsfeld.pdf; Mora memo, p. 15; Jane Mayer, "The Memo," *New Yorker*, February 27, 2006, http://www.newyorker.com/archive/2006/02/27/060227fa_fact; Daniel J. Dell'Orto, Principle Deputy General Counsel of the Department of Defense, "Press Briefing by White House Counsel Judge Alberto Gonzales, DoD General Counsel William Haynes, DoD Deputy General Counsel Daniel Dell'Orto and Army Deputy Chief of Staff for Intelligence General Keith Alexander," White House Press Briefing, June 22, 2004, http://www.whitehouse.gov/news/releases/2004/06/20040622-14.html.

[22] Memorandum from Rumsfeld, Secretary of Defense, to the Commander, US Southern Command, "Counter-Resistance Techniques in the War on Terrorism (S)," April 16, 2003; *Working Group Report on Detainee Interrogations in the Global War on Terrorism: Assessment of Legal, Historical, Policy, and Operational Considerations*, (Department of Defense, April 4, 2003). Memoranda available in *The Torture Papers*, pp. 360-265, 286-359. The Working Group report, which relied in part on the reasoning articulated in the Bybee memorandum, was signed by Rumsfeld and "briefed" to military officials, including Major Geoffrey Miller. Major Miller subsequently was assigned to Iraq to advise officials on interrogating Iraqi detainees. Many of these techniques became part of U.S. interrogation policy and practice in Iraq. Mayer, "The Memo."

[23] Mayer, "The Memo."

[24] *Rasul v. Bush,* 542 U.S. 466 (2004) (holding that detainees at Guantánamo Bay must have access to federal courts to challenge the legality of their detention); *Hamdi v. Rumsfeld*, 542 U.S. 507 (2004) (holding that a U.S. citizen held as an "enemy combatant" must be given a meaningful opportunity to contest the factual basis for that detention before a neutral decision-maker).

[25] Memorandum from Paul Wolfowitz, Deputy Defense Secretary, to the Secretary of the Navy, "Order Establishing Combatant Status Review Tribunal," July 7, 2004, http://www.defenselink.mil/news/Jul2004/d20040707review.pdf. The term "enemy combatant" is defined as "an individual who was part of or supporting Taliban or al Qaeda forces, or associated forces that are engaged in hostilities against the United States or its coalition partners. This includes any person who has committed a belligerent act or has directly supported hostilities in aid of enemy armed forces."

[26] Memorandum from Deputy Secretary of Defense to the Secretaries of Military Departments, et al., "Re: Implementation of Combatant Status Review Tribunal Procedures for Enemy Combatants Detained at U.S. Naval Base Guantánamo Bay, Cuba," July 14, 2006, Enclosure (1), p. 6, G(7), G(11), http://www.defenselink.mil/news/Aug2006/d20060809CSRTProcedures.pdf.

[27] Detainee Treatment Act of 2005, Pub. L. No. 109-148, §1005(b)(1). In fact, the government has specifically declared that CSRT panels may rely on evidence obtained by torture. Appearing before the Supreme Court in *Boumediene v. Bush,* Deputy Associate Attorney General Brian Boyle stated: "If in fact information came to the CSRT's attention that was obtained through a non-traditional means, even torture by a foreign power, I don't think that there is anything in the due process clause even assuming they were [U.S.] citizens. . .that would prevent the CSRT from crediting that information for purposes of sustaining the enemy combatant class." Brian D. Boyle, Principle Deputy Associate Attorney General, Oral Argument Transcript, Dec. 2, 2004, *Khalid v. Bush*, No. 04-1142; *Boumediene v. Bush, et al.,* 04-1166, at 84:7-84:22, cited in Memorandum of Petitioners Zemiri and Al-Marri in Opposition to Motion to Dismiss, *In re* Guantanamo Detainee Cases, No. 04-2046 (D.D.C. Jan. 13, 2005), http://www.pegc.us/archive/Zemiri_v_Bush/zemiri_reply_20050113.pdf.

[28] U. S. Department of Defense, "Combatant Status Review Tribunal Summary," November 2, 2007, http://www.defenselink.mil/news/Nov2007/CSRTUpdate-Nov2-07.pdf (summary of tribunal statistics between July 30, 2004 and June 15, 2007).

[29] *In re* Guantánamo Detainee Cases, 355 F. Supp. 2d 443, 468-69 (D.C. Cir. 2005) (finding that CSRT decisions substantially relied upon classified evidence and that no detainee was ever permitted access to classified information).

[30] Lt. Col. Stephen Abraham, who served in the Office for Administrative Review of Detention of Enemy Combatants from 2004 to 2005, has filed affidavits in two cases outlining the "fundamental flaws" in the CSRT process. Declaration of Lt. Col. Stephen Abraham, U.S. Army Reserve, filed in *Al-Odah, et al v. United States*, No. 06-1196, June 15, 2007, http://www.scotusblog.com/movabletype/archives/2007/06/final_push_for.html; Declaration of Lt. Col. Stephen Abraham, U.S. Army Reserve, filed in *Hamad v. Gates*, 07-1098, November 13, 2007, http://www.scotusblog.com/wp-content/uploads/2007/11/sub-new-abraham-declaration.pdf. *See also* William Glaberson, "Reserve Officer Criticizes Process of Identifying 'Enemy Combatants' at Guantánamo," *New York Times*, June 23, 2007, http://www.nytimes.com/2007/06/23/washington/23combatant.html; Carol D. Leonnig and Josh White, "An Ex-Member Calls Detainee Panels Unfair," *Washington Post*, June 23, 2007, http://www.washingtonpost.com/wp-dyn/content/article/2007/06/22/AR2007062202230.html.

[31] 18 U.S.C. §2441(d)(1)(A); 18 U.S.C. §2340(2).

[32] *Rochin v. California*, 342 U.S. 165, 172 (1952).

[33] *City of Revere v. Mass. Gen. Hospital*, 463 U.S. 239, 244 (1983) (finding that "the due process rights of a [pre-trial detainee] are at least as great as the Eighth Amendment protections available to a convicted prisoner") (*citing Bell v. Wolfish*, 441 U.S. 520, 535 (1979)).

[34] Vice President Dick Cheney, interview by Terry Moran, *Nightline*, ABCNews.com, December 18, 2005, http://www.washingtonpost.com/wp-dyn/content/blog/2008/02/06/BL2008020602244.html.

[35] "Brief on Behalf of Former Federal Judges as Amici Curiae in Support of Petitioners," in al *Odah, et al. v. United States* and *Boumediene, et al. v. Bush*, Nos. 06-1195, 06-1196; *In re* Guantánamo Detainee Cases, 355 F. Supp. 2d at 473 ("it can be reasonably inferred that the CSRT panels did not sufficiently consider whether the evidence upon which the tribunal relied in making its 'enemy combatant' determinations was coerced from the detainees").

[36] Detainee Treatment Act of 2005, Pub. L. No. 109-148, §1005(e)(2)(C)(ii).

[37] *Boumediene, et al. v. Bush*, and *Al-Odah, et al. v. United States*, Nos. 06-1195 & 06-1196.

[38] The administration contends that the Constitution does not apply to detainees at Guantánamo because it is outside the jurisdiction of the United States. *Boumediene v. Bush*, 476 F.3d 981 (D.C. Cir. 2007).

[39] That position was based on the U.S. reservation to Article 16 of CAT, which defines "cruel, inhuman or degrading treatment" as conduct prohibited by the Fifth, Eighth, and Fourteenth Amendments, the protections of which the administration interpreted as inapplicable to "aliens overseas." Alberto Gonzales to Senator Dianne Feinstein, "Responses of Alberto R. Gonzales, Nominee to be Attorney General to the Written Questions of Senator Dianee Feinstein," p. 10 (on file with Human Rights First); Letter from William E. Moschella, Assistant Attorney General, to Senator Patrick J. Leahy, "Re: Obligations of the United States under Article 16 of the U.N. Convention Against Torture," April 4, 2005 (on file with Human Rights First).

[40] *Hamdan v. Rumsfeld*, 126 S. Ct. 2749, 2791-97 (2006); *Rasul v. Bush*, 542 U.S. 466 (2004); *Hamdi v. Rumsfeld*, 542 U.S. 507 (2004).

[41] *Hamdan*, 126 S. Ct. at 2791-97.

[42] Military Commissions Act of 2006, 10 U.S.C. § 948r (c-d); 10 U.S.C. § 949a (b)(2)(C) (further providing that "[a] statement of the accused that is otherwise admissible shall not be excluded from trial by military commission on grounds of alleged coercion or compulsory self-incrimination so long as the evidence complies with the provisions of section 948r of this title"). Proponents of the coerced evidence provisions argued that the evidentiary standards applied in courts-martial and civilian criminal courts were too rigorous and inapplicable to the battlefield and that all terrorism suspects would claim they had been abused. Attorney General Alberto Gonzales, Senate Armed Services Committee, *The Future of Military Commissions in Light of the Supreme Court Decision in Hamdan v. Rumsfeld*, 109th Cong., 2nd sess., 2006; Colonel Morris D. Davis, "In Defense of Guantánamo Bay," 117 Yale L.J. Pocket Part 21 (2007), http://thepocketpart.org/2007/08/13/davis.html. Opponents of the provisions pointed out that permitting the use of coerced evidence during criminal trials was unheard of in our nation's history. Senator John McCain, author of the DTA's prohibition of cruel treatment, said: "I think that if you practice illegal, inhumane treatment and allow that to be admissible in court, that would be a radical departure from any practice [of] this nation." Tom Regan, "Top Military Lawyers Oppose Bush Plan," *Christian Science Monitor*, August 4, 2006, http://www.csmonitor.com/2006/0804/dailyUpdate.html.

[43] 10 U.S.C. § 948r(b).

[44] Brigadier General Thomas Hartmann, Senate Committee on the Judiciary, *The Legal Rights of Guantanamo Detainees: What Are They, Should They Be Changed, and Is an End in Sight?*, 110th Cong., 1st sess., 2007; Josh White, "Evidence From Waterboarding Could Be Used in Military Trials," *Washington Post*, December 12, 2007, http://www.washingtonpost.com/wp-dyn/content/article/2007/12/11/AR2007121102110.html. Reportedly the Bush Administration has cabled U.S. embassies throughout the world with instructions to emphasize that statements obtained through torture will be inadmissible at military commission trials, but that statements obtained through CID may come in to evidence. Josh White, Walter Pincus and Julie Tate, "Rules for Lawyers Of Detainees Are Called Onerous," *Washington Post*, February 13, 2008, http://www.washingtonpost.com/wp-dyn/content/article/2008/02/12/AR2008021203042.html.

[45] Attorney General Michael Mukasey, Senate Committee on the Judiciary, *Oversight of the U.S. Department of Justice*, 110th Cong., 2nd sess., 2008; Dan Eggen, "White House Pushes Waterboarding Rationale," *Washington Post*, February 13, 2008, http://www.washingtonpost.com/wp-dyn/content/article/2008/02/12/AR2008021202691_pf.html.

[46] Assistant Attorney General Steven Bradbury, House Committee on the Judiciary Subcommittee on Constitution, Civil Rights and Civil Liberties, *Justice Department's Office of Legal Counsel*, 110th Cong., 2nd sess., 2008. Testifying before the Senate Intelligence Committee a week earlier, CIA Director Michael Hayden also defended waterboarding: "We used it against these three high-value detainees because of the circumstances of the time. Very critical to those circumstances was the belief that additional catastrophic attacks against the homeland were imminent." CIA Director Michael Hayden, Senate Intelligence Committee, *Current and Projected National Security Threats*, 110th Cong., 2nd sess., 2008; Dan Froomkin, "We Tortured and We'd Do It Again," *Washington Post*, February 6, 2008, http://www.washingtonpost.com/wp-dyn/content/blog/2008/02/06/BL2008020602244.html.

[47] Brigadier General Thomas Hartmann, Department of Defense Press Briefing, February 11, 2008, http://www.defenselink.mil/transcripts/transcript.aspx?transcriptid=4142.

[48] 10 U.S.C. § 949a (b)(2)(E). The relevant language reads:

(E)(i) Except as provided in clause (ii), hearsay evidence not otherwise admissible under the rules of evidence applicable in trial by general courts-martial may be admitted in a trial by military commission if the proponent of the evidence makes known to the adverse party, sufficiently in advance to provide the adverse party with a fair opportunity to meet the evidence, the intention of the proponent to offer the evidence, and the particulars of the evidence (including information on the general circumstances under which the evidence was obtained). The disclosure of evidence under the preceding sentence is subject to the requirements and limitations applicable to the disclosure of classified information in section 949j(c) of this title.

(ii) Hearsay evidence not otherwise admissible under the rules of evidence applicable in trial by general courts-martial shall not be admitted in a trial by military commission if the party opposing the admission of the evidence demonstrates that the evidence is unreliable or lacking in probative value.

[49] 10 U.S.C. § 949d (f)(2)(B). The relevant language reads:

PROTECTION OF SOURCES, METHODS, OR ACTIVITIES- The military judge, upon motion of trial counsel, shall permit trial counsel to introduce otherwise admissible evidence before the military commission, while protecting from disclosure the sources, methods, or activities by which the United States acquired the evidence if the military judge finds that (i) the sources, methods, or activities by which the United States acquired the evidence are classified, and (ii) the evidence is reliable. The military judge may require trial counsel to present to the military commission and the defense, to the extent practicable and consistent with national security, an unclassified summary of the sources, methods, or activities by which the United States acquired the evidence.

[50] Mil. Comm. R. Evid. 304, Discussion.

[51] *U.S. v. Singleterry*, 29 F.3d 733, 737 (1st Cir. 1994) (*citing Opper v. U.S.* 348 U.S. 84, 93 (1954)).

[52] Department of Defense, "Detainee Transfer Announced," U.S. Department of Defense Press Release, December 28, 2007, http://www.defenselink.mil/releases/release.aspx?releaseid=11591.

[53] Department of Defense, "Defense Department Takes Custody Of A High-Value Detainee," U.S. Department of Defense Press Release, March 14, 2008, http://www.defenselink.mil/releases/release.aspx?releaseid=11758; Department of Defense, "Military Commission Charges Referred," U.S. Department of Defense Press Release, January 31, 2008, http://www.defenselink.mil/releases/release.aspx?releaseid=11655.

[54] Five other detainees (Sufyian Barhoumi, Jabran Said Bin al Qahtani, Ghassan Abdullah al Sharbi, Binyam Ahmed Muhammed, and Muhammad Abdul Zahir) were charged under the 2002 military commission scheme, which was held unconstitutional in *Hamdan*. Their cases were suspended and have not been reinstated under the 2006 MCA. U.S. Department of Defense, Military Commissions, "Web Archives," http://www.defenselink.mil/news/commissionsarchives.html (charges for these five detainees are not reinstated and are missing from the current "Commission Cases" webpage, http://www.defenselink.mil/news/commissions.html).

[55] Center for Human Rights and Global Justice at NYU School of Law, Human Rights Watch and Human Rights First, *By the Numbers: Findings of the Detainee Abuse and Accountability Project* (New York: April 2006), http://www.humanrightsfirst.info/pdf/06425-etn-by-the-numbers.pdf.

[56] President George W. Bush, "President Discusses Creation of Military Commissions to Try Suspected Terrorists."

[57] U.S. Department of Defense, Military Commissions Charge Sheet for Khalid Sheikh Mohammed, Walid Muhammad Salih Mubarak Bin 'Attash, Ramzi Binalshibh, Ali Abdul Aziz Ali, Mustafa Ahmed Adam al Hawsawi, and Mohamed al Kahtani, February 11, 2008, http://www.defenselink.mil/news/Feb2008/d20080211chargesheet.pdf (charged with conspiracy, attacking civilians, attacking civilian objects, intentionally causing serious bodily injury, murder in violation of the law of war, destruction of property in violation of the law of war, hijacking or hazarding a vessel or aircraft, terrorism, and providing material support for terrorism).

[58] CIA Director Michael Hayden, Senate (Select) Intelligence Committee, *Current and Projected National Security Threats*, 110th Cong., 2nd sess., 2008.

[59] Ron Suskind, *The One Percent Doctrine* (New York: Simon & Schuster, 2006), pp. 228-230; Brian Ross and Richard Esposito, "CIA's Harsh Interrogation Techniques Described." Mohammed is currently being held, along with fourteen other "high-value" detainees, in a secret location in Guantánamo known as Camp 7. Lawyers who are permitted to speak with Camp 7 detainees require top-secret security clearance and screenings and are forbidden from revealing where the detainees were held by the CIA or how they were interrogated. Carol Rosenberg, "First 9/11 Death Penalty Defendant Gets Military Lawyer," *Miami Herald*, February 12, 2008.

[60] Office of the Director of National Intelligence, *Summary of the High Value Terrorist Detainee Program*, September 2006, www.dni.gov/announcements/content/TheHighValueDetaineeProgram.pdf; President George W. Bush, "President Discusses Creation of Military Commissions to Try Suspected Terrorists."

[61] Suskind, *The One Percent Doctrine*, pp. 229-230; Associated Press, "Khalid Sheikh Mohammed's Words Provide Glimpse into the Mind of a Terrorist," *USA Today*, March 16, 2007, http://www.usatoday.com/news/world/2007-03-16-ksm-psych_N.htm; Elaine Shannon and Michael Weisskopf, "Khalid Sheikh Mohammed Names Names," *Time*, March 24, 2003, http://www.time.com/time/nation/article/0,8599,436061,00.html (reporting that "some officials remain skeptical that at least some of the information he is feeding interrogators is intentionally misleading." However, some of his disclosures were corroborated, leading one counter-terrorism official to characterize the intelligence as, "valuable, credible, specific information").

[62] Suskind, *The One Percent Doctrine*, pp. 229-230. *See infra* Chapter 5 for a discussion of the effects of torture and cruel treatment on detained suspects.

[63] Katherine Schrader, Associated Press, "Officials: Mohammed Exaggerated Claims," *Washington Post*, March 15, 2007, http://www.washingtonpost.com/wp-dyn/content/article/2007/03/15/AR2007031501478.html.

[64] Shannon and Weisskopf, "Khalid Sheikh Mohammed Names Names."

[65] Jane Mayer, "The Black Sites," *New Yorker*, August 13, 2007, http://www.newyorker.com/reporting/2007/08/13/070813fa_fact_mayer/.

[66] *Ibid* (quoting former CIA analyst Bruce Riedel). According to another account, a CIA source said that Mohammed later recanted some of the information he provided under interrogation. Risen, *State of War*, p. 33.

[67] Josh White, Dan Eggen, and Joby Warrick, "U.S. to Try 6 On Capital Charges Over 9/11 Attacks," *Washington Post*, February 12, 2008, http://www.washingtonpost.com/wp-dyn/content/story/2008/02/11/ST2008021101227.html.

[68] *Al-Marri v. Wright*, 487 F.3d 160, 165 (4th Cir. 2007).

[69] Declaration of Mr. Jeffrey N. Rapp, Director, Joint Intelligence Task Force for Combating Terrorism, *Al-Marri v. Hanft*, 378 F. Supp 2d.673, No. 2:04-02257 (D.S.C. April 5, 2006), para. 8, 12-15, http://www.washingtonpost.com/wp-srv/nation/documents/jeffreyrapp_document.pdf. The Defense Department official notes: "This statement is derived from specific intelligence sources. This declaration does not identify the specific source of such information."

[70] *Al-Marri v. Wright*, 487F.3d 160 (4th Cir. June 2007).

[71] President George W. Bush, "President Discusses Creation of Military Commissions to Try Suspected Terrorists."

[72] *Ibid.*

[73] Motion to Declare Interrogation Methods Applied Against Petitioner Constitute Torture, *Majid Khan v. Robert Gates*, No. 07-1324, (D.C. Cir. Dec. 6, 2007).

[74] Motion to Declare Interrogation Methods Applied Against Petitioner Constitute Torture, *Majid Khan v. Robert Gates*, No. 07-1324, (D.C. Cir. Dec. 6, 2007). A United States appeals court has referred the motion to a merits panel. Order, *Majid Khan v. Robert Gates*, No. 07-1324 (D.C. Cir. Feb 14, 2008), http://pacer.cadc.uscourts.gov/cgi-bin/image_pdf.pl?casenum=07-1324&dt=200802&histid=1099104&view=yes&puid=01203972801.

[75] President George W. Bush, "President Discusses Creation of Military Commissions to Try Suspected Terrorists."

[76] At this writing, a military commission judge has permitted lawyers for Salim Ahmed Hamdan to submit written questions to Mohammed asking whether Hamdan took part in the September 11 suicide plot and other attacks. The lawyers, however, are not permitted to inquire about interrogation techniques used on Mohammed. On Reconsideration Ruling on Motion to Stay and for Access to High Value Detainees, *United States v. Salim Ahmed Hamdan*, March 14, 2008, http://www.defenselink.mil/news/Mar2008/d20080314hamdanruling.pdf.

[77] Letter from Marc D. Falkoff to Administrative Review Board, "Re: ARB Hearing for Abd Al Malik Abd al Wahab, ISN 037," April 30, 2005 (on file with Human Rights First).

[78] Letter from Marc D. Falkoff to Administrative Review Board, "Re: ARB Hearing for Faruq Ali Ahmed, ISN 032," February 5, 2005 (on file with Human Rights First).

[79] Letter from Marc D. Falkoff to Administrative Review Board, "Re: ARB Hearing for Uthman Abdul Rahim Mohammed Uthman," June 1, 2005 (on file with Human Rights First).

[80] Office of the Assistant Secretary of Defense (Public Affairs), "Guantánamo Provides Valuable Intelligence Information," U.S. Department of Defense News Release, June 12, 2005, http://www.fas.org/irp/news/2005/06/dod061205.html.

[81] U.S. Department of Defense, Military Commissions Charge Sheet for Khalid Sheikh Mohammed, Walid Muhammad Salih Mubarak Bin 'Attash, Ramzi Binalshibh, Ali Abdul Aziz Ali, Mustafa Ahmed Adam al Hawsawi, Mohamed al Kahtani, February 11, 2008.

[82] Adam Zagorin and Michael Duffy, "Inside the Interrogation of Detainee 063", *Time*, June 12, 2005, http://www.time.com/time/magazine/article/0,9171,1071284,00.html.

[83] Daniel J. Dell'Orto, White House Press Briefing, June 22, 2004.

[84] Bill Dedman, "Can the '20th Hijacker' of Sept. 11 Stand Trial?" MSNBC.com, October 24, 2006, http://www.msnbc.msn.com/id/15361462/.

[85] Lt. Gen. Mark Schmidt and Brig. Gen. John Furlow, *Final Report, Investigation into FBI Allegations of Detainee Abuse at Guantánamo Bay, Cuba Detention Facility*, (U.S. Department of Defense, June 9, 2005), p.14, http://www.defenselink.mil/news/Jul2005/d20050714report.pdf (hereafter "Schmidt-Furlow Report"). Al-Qahtani's entire interrogation log was made public by *Time Magazine* in 2006 (hereafter "Interrogation Log"), http://www.time.com/time/2006/log/log.pdf.

[86] Zagorin and Duffy, "Inside the Interrogation of Detainee 063;" Corine Hegland, "Guantánamo's Grip," *National Journal*, February 3, 2006, http://nationaljournal.com/about/njweekly/stories/2006/0203nj1.htm.

[87] Tim Golden and Don Van Natta Jr., "Most Guantánamo Prisoners of No Strategic Value," *New York Times*, June 21, 2004.

[88] Schmidt-Furlow Report, pp. 7-8, 20 (describes acts of sexual humiliation), 14-15, 27 (concludes that using a dog was unauthorized when used in October 2002).

[89] Schmidt-Furlow Report, p. 19; Adam Zagorin and Michael Duffy, "Inside the Interrogation of Detainee 063," *Time*, June 12, 2005, http://www.time.com/time/magazine/article/0,9171,1071284,00.html; Interrogation Log, p. 47.

[90] Interrogation log, p. 27.

[91] Office of the Assistant Secretary of Defense (Public Affairs), "Guantánamo Provides Valuable Intelligence Information," U.S. Department of Defense News Release, June 12, 2005, http://www.fas.org/irp/news/2005/06/dod061205.html; Daniel J. Dell'Orto, White House Press Briefing, June 22, 2004.

[92] Adam Zagorin, "20th Hijacker' Claims That Torture Made Him Lie," *Time*, March 3, 2006, http://www.time.com/time/nation/article/0,8599,1169322,00.html.

[93] Verbatim transcript of Administrative Review Board hearing for ISN 063 [al-Qahtani], Enclosure (5), p. 8, http://www.dod.mil/pubs/foi/detainees/csrt_arb/ARB_Transcript_2000-2099.pdf.

[94] Dedman, "Can the '20th Hijacker' of Sept. 11 Stand Trial?"

[95] The report concluded that the "creative, aggressive, and persistent interrogation of the subject of the first Special Interrogation Plan resulted in the cumulative effect being degrading and abusive treatment." It also stated that the impact of 48 of 54 consecutive days of 18 to 20-hour interrogations, paired with 160 days of segregation from other detainees, was "particularly troubling." Schmidt-Furlow Report, p. 20.

[96] Suskind, *The One Percent Doctrine*, p. 89; David Johnston, "At a Secret Interrogation, Dispute Flared Over Tactics," *New York Times*, September 10, 2006, http://www.nytimes.com/2006/09/10/washington/10detain.html. During the next several years, Zubaydah was likely transferred to several other secret CIA detention facilities around the world, possibly including facilities in Poland, Diego Garcia and Africa. The interrogations continued in these facilities. Council of Europe, Parliamentary Assembly, Committee on Legal Affairs and Human Rights, *Secret detentions and illegal transfers of detainees involving Council of Europe member states: second report*, prepared by Rapporteur Dick Marty, June 7, 2007, http://assembly.coe.int/CommitteeDocs/2007/EMarty_20070608_NoEmbargo.pdf.

[97] David Johnston, "At a Secret Interrogation, Dispute Flared Over Tactics," *New York Times*, September 10, 2006, http://www.nytimes.com/2006/09/10/washington/10detain.html; Katherine Eban, "Rorschach and Awe," Vanity Fair.com, July 17, 2007, http://www.vanityfair.com/politics/features/2007/07/torture200707; Risen, *State of War*, pp. 20-23; Suskind, *The One Percent Doctrine*, p. 115 (reporting that "test[ing] boundaries" began in May 2002).

[98] Johnston, "At a Secret Interrogation, Dispute Flared Over Tactics."

[99] Richard Esposito and Brian Ross, "Coming in From the Cold: CIA Spy Calls Waterboarding Necessary But Torture," ABCNews.com, December 10, 2007 (discussing interview with John Kiriakou featured on *World News With Charles Gibson* and *Nightline*); Johnston, "At a Secret Interrogation, Dispute Flared Over Tactics."

[100] President George W. Bush, "President Discusses Creation of Military Commissions to Try Suspected Terrorists."

[101] H.R. 4951, 108th Cong., (2004) (To require the videotaping of interrogations and other pertinent actions between a detainee or prisoner in the custody or under the effective control of the armed forces of the United States pursuant to an interrogation, or other pertinent interaction, for the purpose of gathering intelligence and a member of the armed forces of the United States, an intelligence operative of the United States, or a contractor of the United States).

[102] *Army Field Manual 2-22*.3, sec. 9-29.

[103] CIA Director Michael Hayden, Senate (Select) Intelligence Committee, *Current and Projected National Security Threats*, 110th Cong., 2nd sess., 2008.

[104] Johnston, "At a Secret Interrogation, Dispute Flared Over Tactics."

[105] Brian Ross, "Sources Tell ABC News Top al Qaeda Figures Held in CIA Secret Prisons," ABCNews.com, December 5, 2005, http://abcnews.go.com/WNT/Investigation/story?id=1375123.

[106] Suskind, p. 115. *See also* Eban, "Rorschach and Awe;" Mayer, "The Black Sites," (reporting that Zubaydah informed the ICRC that he had been placed in a "dog box"—a small cage—for lengthy periods of time).

[107] Mark Mazzetti and David Johnson, "Inquiry Begins Into Destruction of Tapes," *New York Times*, December 9, 2007, http://www.nytimes.com/2007/12/09/washington/09zubaydah.html?_r=1&oref=slogin.

[108] Mark Mazzetti and Scott Shane, "Destruction of C.I.A. Tapes Cleared by Lawyers," *New York Times*, December 11, 2007, http://www.nytimes.com/2007/12/11/washington/11intel.html?ex=1355029200&en=260ed8b0c9e0df0d&ei=5088&partner=rssnyt&emc=rss.

[109] Mark Mazzetti, "C.I.A. Destroyed Tapes of Interrogations," *New York Times*, December 6, 2007, http://www.nytimes.com/2007/12/06/washington/06cnd-intel.html; Warren Richey, "Destroyed CIA Tapes Spur Probes," *Christian Science Monitor*, December 10, 2007, http://www.csmonitor.com/2007/1210/p03s03-usju.html?page=1.

[110] In February 2008, Zubaydah's lawyers filed a petition for his release in the D.C. Circuit Court of Appeals, arguing that his "prolonged, indefinite and restrictive detention" violates both domestic and international law. Amended Petition for Relief Under the Detainee Treatment Act of 2005, and, in the Alternative, for Writ of Habeas Corpus, *Zayn Al Abidin Muhammad Husayn v. Robert M. Gates*, No. 07-1520, (D.C. Cir. Feb. 21, 2008).

[111] Esposito and Ross, "Coming in From the Cold: CIA Spy Calls Waterboarding Necessary But Torture."

[112] Verbatim Transcript of Combatant Status Review Tribunal Hearing for ISN 10016 [Abu Zubaydah], March 27, 2007, p. 24, http://www.defenselink.mil/news/transcript_ISN10016.pdf.

[113] Eggen and Pincus, "FBI, CIA Debate Significance of Terror Suspect." Journalist Ron Suskind reported that Zubyadah suffered from multiple personality disorder, calling into question his general credibility. *The Washington Times* cited a counterterrorism official who disagrees with Suskind's account of Zubyadah's mental state, however, questioning the veracity of Suskind's information, calling Zubyadah "'crazy like a fox,'" and maintaining that Zubaydah did provide important information. Ron Suskind, "The Unofficial Story of the al-Qaeda 14," *Time*, September 10, 2006, http://www.time.com/time/magazine/article/0,9171,1533436,00.html; Suskind, *The One Percent,Doctrine*, pp. 95, 100-101; Bill Gertz and Rowan Scarborough, "Inside the Ring," *Washington Times*, June 23, 2006, http://www.gertzfile.com/gertzfile/ring062306.html.

[114] Mazzetti and Johnston, "Inquiry Begins Into Destruction of Tapes." Zubaydah was also the primary source for the material witness warrant issued for the arrest of Jose Padilla in May 2002. When Padilla was finally prosecuted in federal court in 2007, his lawyers claimed that Zubaydah had implicated Padilla while suffering from gunshot wounds and possibly without adequate medication. Jose Padilla's Motion to Suppress Physical Evidence And Issue Writs Ad Testificandum, *U.S. v. Jose Padilla, et al.*, No. 04-60001, (S.D.FLA May 2006), at 3-4, http://jurist.law.pitt.edu/ControvertWarrantSuppressEvidenceMotion.pdf. But the Justice Department contended there was no evidence that Zubaydah had

been tortured. Emily Bazelon and Dahlia Lithwick, "If the CIA Hadn't Destroyed those Tapes, What Would Be Different?" *Slate*, December 10, 2007, http://www.slate.com/id/2179607/.

[115] National Commission on Terrorist Attacks Upon the United States, *The 9/11 Commission Report* (New York: W.W. Nortan and Company, 2004), pp. 165-66, http://www.9-11commission.gov/report/911Report_Ch5.pdf; Dana Priest and Scott Higham, "At Guantánamo: A Prison Within a Prison," *Washington Post*, December 17, 2004, http://www.washingtonpost.com/ac2/wp-dyn/A5918-2004Dec16?language=printer.

[116] Jess Bravin, "The Conscience of the Colonel," *Wall Street Journal*, March 31, 2007; Schmidt-Furlow Report, pp. 21-25.

[117] Bravin, "The Conscience of the Colonel."

[118] Schmidt-Furlow Report, p. 25.

[119] *Ibid.*

[120] Col. Morris D. Davis, "AWOL Military Justice," *Los Angeles Times*, December 10, 2007, http://www.latimes.com/news/printedition/asection/la-oe-davis10dec10,1,743034.story. *See also* Col. Morris D. Davis, "Military Commissions: Fair or Foul?," *Los Angeles Times*, December 26, 2007, http://www.latimes.com/news/opinion/la-oew-morris26dec26,0,7831090.story.

[121] E-mail from Capt. John Carr to Col. Fred Borch, "Re: Meeting with Colonel Borch and Myself, 4:00 p.m. Today, Col. Borch's Office," March 15, 2004, (on file with Human Rights First); E-mail from Maj. Robert Preston to Capt. Teresa Davenport, "Re: Meeting with Colonel Borch and Myself, 4:00 p.m. Today, Col. Borch's Office," March 11, 2004, (on file with Human Rights First). *See also* Jess Bravin, "Two Prosecutors Quit in Protest," *Wall Street Journal*, August 1, 2005. A Defense Department Inspector General investigation, however, did not substantiate the allegations. Office of Assistant Inspector General for Investigations, *PROJECT: Military Commission (MILCOM)*, (April 30, 2004), p. 30, http://www.dodig.osd.mil/fo/foia/ERR/r_REDACTED-MILCOM-ROIonly.pdf.

[122] E-mail from Capt. John Carr to Col. Fred Borch, "Re: Meeting with Colonel Borch and Myself," March 15, 2004.

[123] *Ibid.*; E-mail from Maj. Robert Preston to Capt. Teresa Davenport, "Re: Meeting with Colonel Borch and Myself," March 11, 2004. Maj. Preston's e-mail adds: "I sincerely believe that this process is wrongly managed, wrongly focused and a blight on the reputation of the armed forces." Later he states: "I lie a wake worrying about this every night. I find it almost impossible to focus on my part of the mission—after all, writing a motion saying that the process will be full and fair when you don't really believe it will be is kind of hard—particularly when you want to call yourself an officer and a lawyer. This assignment is quite literally ruining my life."

[124] Jess Bravin, "Dispute Stymies Guantanamo Terror Trials," *Wall Street Journal*, September 26, 2007.

[125] Josh White, "Pressure Alleged in Detainee Hearings," *Washington Post*, October 21, 2007, http://www.washingtonpost.com/wp-dyn/content/article/2007/10/20/AR2007102001002.html; William Glaberson, "Claim of Pressure for Closed Guantánamo Trials," *New York Times*, October 22, 2007, http://www.nytimes.com/2007/10/20/us/nationalspecial3/20gitmo.html.

[126] Ben Fox, "Ex-Prosecutor to Serve as Defense Witness in Terror Case," *Washington Post*, February 22, 2008, http://www.washingtonpost.com/wp-dyn/content/article/2008/02/21/AR2008022102662.html.

[127] Jane Sutton, "Ex-Guantanamo prosecutor to leave U.S. military," *Reuters*, March 25, 2008, http://www.reuters.com/article/reutersEdge/idUSN3P38816520080325.

[128] *Ibid.*

[129] *Ibid.*

[130] Bravin, "The Conscience of the Colonel."

[131] *Ibid;.* Letter from Mohamedou Ould Slahi to Nancy Hollander and Sylvia Royce, November 9, 2006, http://online.wsj.com/public/resources/documents/couch-slahiletter-03312007.pdf.

[132] Bravin, "The Conscience of the Colonel."

[133] Mohamed alleges that he was first taken to Landi prison in Pakistan and held there from April 13-20, 2002, where he was not interrogated. He was taken a week later to the I.C.I. unit, a Karachi interrogation center. Memorandum from Attorney Clive Stafford Smith, "Binyam Mohammed al-Habashi," August 1, 2005 (on file with Human Rights First); Brief of Binyam Mohammed as Amicus Curiae in Support of Petitioner, *Hamdan v. Rumsfeld*, 126 S. Ct. 2749 (2006) (No. 05-184) at 3, http://www.hamdanvrumsfeld.com/MohammedAmicusFinal.pdf. *See also* Written evidence submitted by Reprieve: British Involvement in Renditions and Torture, As part of the House of Commons Foreign Affairs—Fourth Report, Case 2: Binyam Mohammed Al-Habashi, March 2006, http://www.publications.parliament.uk/pa/cm200506/cmselect/cmfaff/573/573we25.htm.

[134] Memorandum from Attorney Clive Stafford Smith, "Binyam Mohammed al-Habashi;" Brief of Binyam Mohammed as Amicus Curiae in Support of Petitioner, *Hamdan v. Rumsfeld*, 126 S. Ct. 2749 (2006) (No. 05-184) at 3.

[135] Andrew Selsky, Associated Press, "Gitmo Inmate's Lawyer Urges U.S. on Photos," *USA Today*, December 10, 2007, http://www.usatoday.com/news/topstories/2007-12-10-3587204980_x.htm. Smith maintains that U.S. officials continued to abuse Mohamed after his

arrival at Guantánamo Bay, and Mohamed's mental health has deteriorated as a result. Robert Verkaik, "UK Guantánamo Detainee Near Suicide After Years of Torture, Doctors Warn," *The Independent*, December 18, 2007, http://www.independent.co.uk/news/world/americas/uk-guantanamo-detainee-near-suicide-after-years-of-torture-doctors-warn-765686.html.

[136] Brief of Binyam Mohammed as Amicus Curiae in Support of Petitioner, *Hamdan v. Rumsfeld*, 126 S. Ct. 2749 (2006) (No. 05-184) at 7-9, http://www.hamdanvrumsfeld.com/MohammedAmicusFinal.pdf; Memorandum from Attorney Clive Stafford Smith, "Binyam Mohammed al-Habashi," pp. 13-20..

[137] Brief of Binyam Mohammed as Amicus Curiae in Support of Petitioner, *Hamdan v. Rumsfeld*, 126 S. Ct. 2749 (2006), (No. 05-184), at 10, http://www.hamdanvrumsfeld.com/MohammedAmicusFinal.pdf; Memorandum from Attorney Clive Stafford Smith, "Binyam Mohammed al-Habashi," pp. 20-22.

[138] Memorandum from Attorney Clive Stafford Smith, "Binyam Mohammed al-Habashi," pp. 22-24.

[139] United States of America v. Binyam Ahmed Muhammad, U.S. Department of Defense Charge Sheet, Military Commission Case No. 05-0009, November 4, 2005, para 14, http://www.defenselink.mil/news/Nov2005/d20051104muhammad.pdf; *United States v. Binyam Ahmed Muhammad*, U.S. Department of Defense Referral, Military Commission Case No. 05-0009, December 12, 2005, http://www.defenselink.mil/news/Dec2005/d20051220muhammadreferral.pdf. Mohamed had an initial hearing before a military commission on April 6, 2006. For a brief description, see Priti Patel, "Muhammad Challenges the Commissions; His Lawyer Raises an Ethical Objection and Pleads the Fifth," Human Rights First Blog, April 6, 2006, http://www.humanrightsfirst.org/us_law/detainees/gitmo_diary/post-040606-patel.asp.

[140] Clive Stafford Smith, phone interview by Human Rights First, March 13, 2007.

[141] Carol Rosenberg, "Lawyer Seeks Britain's Help in Preserving Guantánamo Evidence," *Miami Herald*, December 10, 2007; Selsky, "Gitmo Inmate's Lawyer Urges U.S. on Photos."

[142] Jess Bravin, "As Justices Weigh Military Tribunals, A Guantánamo Tale," *Wall Street Journal*, March 28, 2006, p. A1 (a useful comparison of the two men's treatment in the U.S. legal and extra-legal systems); Deputy Attorney General James Comey, interview by Wolf Blitzer, "Justice Department Briefing on Jose Padilla," CNN.com Transcript, June 1, 2004, http://transcripts.cnn.com/TRANSCRIPTS/0406/01/se.02.html.

[143] Motion to Dismiss for Outrageous Government Conduct, *U.S. v. Padilla*, et al., No. 04-6001 (S.D.Fla Oct. 04, 2006), at 2-5; "Expected Testimony Regarding Jose Mr. Padilla," Stuart Grassain, M.D., *U.S. v. Padilla*, et al., No. 04-60001 (S.D.Fla March 07, 2007) at 11. According to psychiatric assessments, the totality of abuse Padilla suffered, especially his prolonged confinement, had a significant impact on his mental health. Padilla's lawyers questioned his mental competency and moved to dismiss his case based upon his allegations of torture and abuse. But their motion was denied. Order Denying Defendant Padilla's Motion to Dismiss for Outrageous Government Conduct, *U.S. v. Jose Padilla*, et al., No. 04-60001 (S.D.Fla April 9, 2007), http://www.discourse.net/archives/docs/Padilla-motion-denied.pdf.

[144] Deputy Attorney General James Comey, interview by Wolf Blitzer, June 1, 2004.

[145] Superseding Indictment, *U.S. v. Hassoun*, No. 04-60001 (S.D.Fla Nov. 17, 2005) at 3, news.findlaw.com/nytimes/docs/padilla/uspad111705ind.pdf; Department of Justice, "Jose Padilla Charged With Conspiracy To Murder Individuals Overseas, Providing Material Support To Terrorists," U.S. Department of Justice Press Release, November 22, 2005, http://www.usdoj.gov/opa/pr/2005/November/05_crm_624.html.

[146] Robert Verkaik, "Guantánamo 'Show Trial' Looms for UK Resident", *The Independent*, February 16, 2008, http://www.independent.co.uk/news/uk/home-news/guantanamo-show-trial-looms-for-uk-resident-782988.html.

[147] *Ibid.*

[148] *O.K. v. Bush*, 377 F. Supp. 2d 102, 103 (D.D.C. 2005).

[149] Charges and Specifications, *U.S. v. Khadr*, April 5, 2007, http://www.defenselink.mil/news/Apr2007/KhadrReferral.pdf.

[150] Decl. of Muneer I. Ahmad, Counsel for Petitioner *O.K. v. Bush*, 377 F. Supp. 2d 102, No. 04-1136 (D.D.C. 2005), Exhibit A to Motion for Preliminary Injunction; Affidavit of Omar Ahmed Khadr, Defense Motion To Compel Discovery (Documents Relating to Investigation and Prosecution of Sgt [Redacted], USA), *U.S. v. Omar Khadr*, No. 0766 by Military Commission (Motion Session March 13, 2008), http://www.defenselink.mil/news/Mar2008/d20080313khadrmotions.

[151] *Ibid*, para. 16-17; Affidavit of Omar Ahmed Khadr, Defense Motion To Compel Discovery (Documents Relating to Investigation and Prosecution of Sgt [Redacted], USA), *U.S. v. Omar Khadr*, No. 0766 by Military Commission (Motion Session March 13, 2008), http://www.defenselink.mil/news/Mar2008/d20080313khadrmotions.

[152] *Ibid*, para. 9-12.

[153] Affidavit of Omar Ahmed Khadr, Defense Motion To Compel Discovery (Documents Relating to Investigation and Prosecution of Sgt [Redacted], USA), *U.S. v. Omar Khadr*, No. 0766 by Military Commission (Motion Session March 13, 2008), http://www.defenselink.mil/news/Mar2008/d20080313khadrmotions.

[154] *Ibid*, para. 21.

[155] Decl. of Eric W. Trupin, Ph.D., *O.K. v. Bush*, 377 F. Supp. 2d 102, No. 04 -1136 (D.D.C. 2005), Exhibit B to Motion for Preliminary Injunction, at para. 19. Dr. Eric Trupin found that Khadr's symptoms are "consistent with those exhibited by victims of torture and abuse." *Ibid*, para 24. Trupin further explained that "[i]f left untreated, post-traumatic stress disorder, particularly in juveniles, may cause irreparable damage." *Ibid*, para. 21. Based on Khadr's symptoms and previous accounts of attempted suicide, Trupin labeled Khadr "at a moderate to high risk for suicide." *Ibid*, para. 23.

[156] Defense Motion For Dismissal Due to Lack of Jurisdiction Under the MCA in Regard to Juvenile Crimes of a Child Soldier, *U.S. v. Omar Khadr*, No. 0766 by Military Commission (Motion Session Feb 4-8, 2008), http://www.nimj.org/documents/Khadr%20Child%20Soldier%20Motion%20to%20Dismiss.pdf.

[157] Defense Motion To Compel Discovery (Documents Relating to Investigation and Prosecution of Sgt [Redacted], USA), *U.S. v. Omar Khadr*, No. 0766 by Military Commission (Motion Session March 13, 2008), http://www.defenselink.mil/news/Mar2008/d20080313khadrmotions.pdf.

[158] William Glaberson, "Witness Names to Be Withheld From Detainee," *New York Times*, December 1, 2007; William Glaberson, "Decks Are Stacked in War Crimes Cases, Lawyers Say," *New York Times*, November 8, 2007; Carol Rosenberg, "Detainee arraigned, says he was abused," *Miami Herald*, March 14, 2008, http://www.miamiherald.com/news/nation/story/456004.html.

[159] *Malloy v. Hogan*, 378 U.S. 1, 8 (1964).

[160] *Schneckloth v. Bustamante*, 412 U.S. 218, 225 (1973); *Lego v. Twomey*, 404 U.S. 477, 489 (1972) (where the voluntariness of a confession is challenged, "the prosecution must prove by at least a preponderance of the evidence that the confession was voluntary"). *See also Colorado v. Connelly*, 479 U.S. 157, 168 (1986) (affirming *Lego*); *Hutto v. Ross*, 429 U.S. 28, 30 (1976) (The test is whether the confession was "'extracted by any sort of threats or violence, (or) obtained by any direct or implied promises, however slight, (or) by the exertion of any improper influence.'"), *citing Bram v. United States*, 168 U.S. 532, 542-43 (1897).

[161] *Ashcraft v. Tennessee*, 322 U.S. 143, 155-56 (1944).

[162] Uniform Code of Military Justice, 10 U.S.C. § 831, Art. 31.

[163] Army Regulation §190-8 ¶2-1.a(1)(d) ("Prisoners may be interrogated in the combat zone. The use of physical or mental torture or any coercion to compel prisoners to provide information is prohibited. Prisoners may voluntarily cooperate with PYSOP [Psychological Operations] personnel in the development, evaluation, or dissemination of PYSOP messages or products. Prisoners may not be threatened, insulted, or exposed to unpleasant or disparate treatment of any kind because of their refusal to answer questions").

[164] *Schneckloth*, 412 U.S. at 226 (assessment includes evaluation of the characteristics of the accused and the details of the interrogation); *Haynes v. Washington*, 373 U.S. 503, 513 (1963).

[165] *Brooks v. Florida*, 389 U.S. 413, 414-15 (1967) (confession involuntary where defendant was held in solitary confinement for 14 days, fed minimal food rations, forced to be naked, and saw no one from outside prison); *Haynes v Washington*, 373 U.S. 503, 514-15 (1963) (confession violated due process where secured after holding defendant for up to seven days in incommunicado detention and promising access to wife and counsel upon confession); *Chambers v. Florida*, 309 U.S. 227, 237-40 (1940) (confession deemed compelled where petitioners were held incommunicado and interrogation, which was conducted with "relentless tenacity," lasted for five days ending with an all night interrogation session); *United States v. Koch*, 552 F.2d 1216, 1219-20 (7th Cir. 1977) (statements were involuntary where defendant confessed only after being placed in solitary confinement in a "boxcar" cell and told he would be transferred to regular segregation if he cooperated); *Townsend v. Henderson*, 405 F.2d 324, 327-29 (6th Cir. 1968) (an inmate's alleged confession was inadmissible because it was involuntarily made to the warden while in solitary confinement and without notice of his constitutional rights regarding custodial interrogation).

[166] *Clewis v. Texas*, 386 U.S. 707, 711-12 (1967) (confession deemed involuntary where defendant was interrogated intermittently for 38 hours, and his faculties were impaired by inadequate sleep, food, and sickness); *Ashcraft v. Tennessee*, 322 U.S. 143, 153 (1944) (confession coerced where defendant was held incommunicado and interrogated for 36 hours without any respite from questioning and with no sleep; *Chambers*, 309 U.S. at 237-238 (interrogation lasted for five days ending with an all night interrogation session).

[167] *Beecher v. Alabama*, 389 U.S. 35, 38-39 (1967) (confession involuntary when police shot suspect in the leg and fired a gun near his head, threatening him with death if he did not tell "the truth.").

[168] *White v. Texas*, 310 U.S. 530 (1940) (confession involuntary where defendant was repeatedly interrogated for 6-7 days and whipped on several successive nights); *Brown v Mississippi*, 297 U.S. 278, 283-86 (1936) (confessions coerced from one defendant who was whipped and hung by a rope to a tree and two others who were stripped naked and whipped).

[169] *Malinski v. New York*, 324 U.S. 401, 405 (1945) (confession involuntary where defendant held for three days incommunicado, and was kept naked in a hotel room for three hours, then provided a blanket for seven more hours); *Brooks v. Florida*, 389 U.S. at 414-15.

[170] *See infra* Chapter 2 for a discussion of the MCA.

[171] *Rogers v. Richmond*, 365 U.S. 534, 540-41 (1961). *See also Rochin v. California*, 342 U.S. 165, 173 (1952) ("Coerced confessions offend the community's sense of fair play and decency"); *Lyons v. Oklahoma*, 322 U.S. 596, 605 (1944). ("A coerced confession is offensive to basic standards of justice, not because the victim has a legal grievance against the police, but because declarations procured by torture are not premises from which a civilized forum will infer guilt.")

¹⁷² *Jackson v. Denno*, 378 U.S. 368, 386 (1964) (quotations omitted), *citing Blackburn v. Alabama*, 361 U.S. 199, 206-07 (1960).

¹⁷³ *Ibid*, quoting *Spano v. New York*, 360 U.S. 315, 320-21 (1959).

¹⁷⁴ *Chambers*, 309 U.S. at 240-41.

¹⁷⁵ *Jackson*, 378 U.S. at 385-86 (noting "the probable unreliability of confessions that are obtained in a manner deemed coercive.").

¹⁷⁶ *Rochin*, 342 U.S. at 173 (coerced confessions "are inadmissible under the Due Process Clause even though the statements contained in them may be independently established as true. Coerced confessions offend the community's sense of fair play and decency.").

¹⁷⁷ *Stein v. New York*, 346 U.S. 156, 200 (1953) (Frankfurter, J., dissenting).

¹⁷⁸ Convention Against Torture, Art. 15, June 26, 1987. The Committee against Torture has made clear that the prohibition applies to both statements of the accused and third-parties and that it applies "to any court or non-court proceedings, particularly penal or administrative proceedings." *P.E. v. France*, Communication No. 193/2001, ¶¶ 3.2 & 3.3 (Dec. 19, 2002).

¹⁷⁹ Article 7 provides in part: "No one shall be subjected to torture or to cruel, inhuman or degrading treatment or punishment." *See also* Article 9 ("Everyone has the right to liberty and security of person. No one shall be subjected to arbitrary arrest or detention. No one shall be deprived of his liberty except on such grounds and in accordance with such procedure as are established by law."); Article 10 ("All persons deprived of their liberty shall be treated with humanity and with respect for the inherent dignity of the human person."). The Human Rights Committee notes that Article 10 applies to "prisons, hospitals—particularly psychiatric hospitals—detention camps or correctional institutions or elsewhere. States parties should ensure that the principle stipulated therein is observed in all institutions and establishments within their jurisdiction where persons are being held." Human Rights Committee, General comment 21 to Article 10.

¹⁸⁰ General Comment 20, para. 12. The Human Rights Committee adds: "[I]t is not sufficient for the implementation of article 7 to prohibit such treatment or punishment or to make it a crime. States parties should inform the Committee of the legislative, administrative, judicial and other measures they take to prevent and punish acts of torture and cruel, inhuman and degrading treatment in any territory under their jurisdiction." General Comment 20, para. 8. *See also Paul v. Republic of Guyana*, Communication No. 728/1996, ¶ 9.3 (Dec. 12, 2001). In addition, Article 14(3)(g) of the ICCPR provides that a criminal suspect is entitled "not to be compelled to testify against himself or to confess guilt." The Human Rights Committee warns that abusive methods are often used in compelling people to confess, and that "the law should require that evidence provided by means of such methods or any other form of compulsion is wholly unacceptable."

¹⁸¹ Common Article 3(1)(d).

¹⁸² *Hamdan*, 126 S. Ct. at 2796-98 (Stevens, J., plurality).

¹⁸³ Protocol I, Art. 75(4)(f).

¹⁸⁴ 18 U.S.C. § 2441 (1997).

¹⁸⁵ *Trial of Sawada*, Case No. 25, 5 Law Reports of Trials of War Criminals at 1, 2 (1948). United Nations guidelines for prosecutors similarly require them to refrain from prosecuting cases based on evidence obtained from torture and cruel treatment. Eighth United Nations Congress on the Prevention of Crime and the Treatment of Offenders, Guidelines on the Role of Prosecutors, Havana, Cuba, Aug. 27-Sept. 7, 1990, Guideline 16 ("When prosecutors come into possession of evidence against suspects that they know or believe on reasonable grounds was obtained through recourse to unlawful methods, which constitute a grave violation of the suspect's human rights, especially involving torture or cruel, inhuman or degrading treatment or punishment, or other abuses of human rights, they shall refuse to use such evidence against anyone other than those who used such methods, or inform the Court accordingly, and shall take all necessary steps to ensure that those responsible for using such methods are brought to justice.").

¹⁸⁶ 18 U.S.C. § 2441(d) (2006).

¹⁸⁷ Rebecca Lemov, *The World as Laboratory: Experiments with Mice, Mazes and Men* (New York: Hill and Wang, 2005), p. 192. *See also* Rebecca Lemov, "The American Science of Interrogation," *Los Angeles Times*, October 22, 2005; Alfred McCoy, "Cruel Science: CIA Torture and U.S. Foreign Policy," *New England Journal of Public Policy*, 19, no. 2, Winter 2005, p. 216.

¹⁸⁸ Robert J. Lifton, "Home by Ship: Reaction Patters of American Prisoners of War Repatriated from North Korea," *American Journal of Psychiatry* April 1954, pp. 733-34; Lemov, "The American Science of Interrogation;" Joost A.M. Meerloo, *The Rape of the Mind: The Psychology of Thought Control, Menticide, and Brainwashin*, (1956), Ch. 1, p. 9, http://www.ninehundred.net/control/. Joost states that the systematic and repetitive use of cruel treatment, exposure to severe temperatures, food deprivation and intimidation over the course of weeks render people suspicious of their own memories and highly susceptible to providing false confessions. He describes the case of U.S. Marine Col. Frank H. Schwable, whose was tortured by the Chinese during the Korean War. Col. Schwable signed a confession stating that the United States waged bacteriological weapons in the Korean War, but he later disavowed the confession. *Ibid*, pp. 8-10.

¹⁸⁹ Lemov, *The World as Laboratory: Experiments with Mice, Mazes and Men*, p. 198.

¹⁹⁰ Lawrence E. Hinkle, Jr., "The Physiological State of the Interrogation Subject as it Affects Brain Function," *The Manipulation of Human Behavior*, ed. Albert D. Biderman and Herbert Zimmer (New York: John Wiley and Sons, Inc., 1961) p. 43, cited in Steven M. Kleinman, "KUBARK Counterintelligence

Interrogation Review: Observations of an Interrogator," *Educing Information: Interrogation: Science and Art: Intelligence Science Board Study Report on Educing Information, Phase 1* (Washington, DC: National Defense Intelligence College Press, September 2006), p. 132.

[191] Lemov, "The American Science of Interrogation."

[192] A thorough discussion of the devastating psychiatric effects of many of the CIA's enhanced interrogation techniques may be found in Human Rights First and Physicians for Human Rights, *Leave No Marks: Enhanced Interrogation Techniques and the Risk of Criminality* (New York: Human Rights First and Physicians for Human Rights, August 2007), http://www.humanrightsfirst.info/pdf/07801-etn-leave-no-marks.pdf.

[193] Randy Borum, "Approaching Truth: Behavioral Science Lessons on Educing Information from Human Sources," *Educing Information: Interrogation: Science and Art: Intelligence Science Board Study Report on Educing Information, Phase 1* (Washington, DC: National Defense Intelligence College Press, September 2006), pp. 26, 42. It is worth noting, however, that Borum also found that almost none of the interrogation techniques employed by U.S. forces over the past 50 years were derived from scientific research or submitted to systematic analysis.

[194] *Ibid*, p. 42. In assessing the claims from some interrogators that coercion has been effectively used to obtain useful information from resistant sources, Col. Steven Kleinman characterizes them as "at best, anecdotal in nature and would be, in the author's view, unlikely to withstand the rigors of sound scientific inquiry." Kleinman, "KUBARK Counterintelligence Interrogation Review: Observations of an Interrogator," fn 71.

[195] Borum, "Approaching Truth: Behavioral Science Lessons on Educing Information from Human Sources," p. 42.

[196] The scientific community is not universal in its condemnation of these practices. Some who have studied the issue suggest that it has not been scientifically determined whether coercive interrogation techniques elicit more or less reliable information than "rapport-based" techniques. M. Gregg Bloche and Jonathan H. Marks, "Doctors and Interrogators at Guantánamo Bay," *New England Journal of Medicine* 353 (July 7, 2005) pp. 6-8, http://www.zmag.org/content/showarticle.cfm?ItemID=8163. In addition, psychiatrists and psychologists played key roles in coercive interrogations at Guantánamo Bay and in CIA interrogations of "high value" detainees, often working as part of "Behavioral Science Consultation Teams" (BSCTs). For a description of the role of the psychiatrists and psychologists in interrogations, *see* Jane Mayer, "The Experiment," *New Yorker*, July 11 & 18, 2005, http://www.newyorker.com/archive/2005/07/11/050711fa_fact4; Drake Bennet, "The War in the Mind," *Boston Globe*, November 27, 2005, http://www.boston.com/news/globe/ideas/articles/2005/11/27/the_war_in_the_mind/. *See also* U.S. Department of Defense, Office of the Inspector General, *Review of DoD-Directed Investigations of Detainee Abuse*, Report No. 06-Intel-10, August 25, 2006, p. 25, http//www.dodig.mil/fo/foia/DetaineeAbuse.html (hereafter "DoD, *Review of Detainee Abuse*").

[197] Borum, "Approaching Truth: Behavioral Science Lessons on Educing Information from Human Sources," p. 42.

[198] Kleinman, "KUBARK Counterintelligence Interrogation Review: Observations of an Interrogator," p.128.

[199] Steven M. Kleinman, phone interview by Human Rights First, March 16, 2007. Kleinman writes in the Intelligence Science Board report that "the scientific community has never established that coercive interrogation methods are an effective means of obtaining reliable intelligence information. In essence, there seems to be an unsubstantiated assumption that 'compliance' carries the same connotation as 'meaningful cooperation' (i.e., a source induced to provide accurate, relevant information of potential intelligence value)." Kleinman, "KUBARK Counterintelligence Interrogation Review: Observations of an Interrogator," p. 126.

[200] Steven A. Drizin and Richard A. Leo, "The Problem of False Confessions in the Post-DNA World," 82 N.C. L. Rev. 891, pp. 948-49, (describing studies that found more than 90% of normal interrogations last less than two hours but that the average length of interrogations that induced false confessions was 16.3 hours).

[201] Bennett, "The War in the Mind." The article describes an experiment that Professor Kassin set up in which college students and police investigators were asked to judge video and audio-taped prisoner confessions. Although the police were more confident in their judgments than the college students, they were more often wrong. *See also* Saul M. Kassin and Lawrence S. Wrightman, "Confession Evidence," in *The Psychology of Evidence and Trial Procedure*, eds. Saul M. Kassin and Lawrence S. Wrightman (Beverly Hills: Sage Publications 1985), pp. 67, 76-80 (reviewing anecdotes and cases histories of false confessions and attributing many of them to coercion).

[202] Drizin and Leo, "The Problem of False Confessions," pp. 921-22 (noting that police and prosecutors rarely consider that a suspect who confessed falsely may be innocent, that prosecutors levy more and higher charges against those who have confessed, that defense lawyers are more likely to advise their clients who have confessed to seek plea bargains, and that judges are conditioned not to believe claims of innocence and rarely suppress confessions).

[203] *Ibid*, pp. 59-61. The article also refers to a previous study with similar results: a 1998 study found that of sampled false confessors who chose to take their case to trial, 73 percent were wrongfully convicted.

[204] Kleinman," KUBARK Counterintelligence Interrogation Review: Observations of an Interrogator," p. 132.

[205] Mayer, "The Experiment;" M. Gregg Bloche and Jonathon H. Marks, "Interrogation: Doing Unto Others as They Did Unto Us," *New York Times*, November 14, 2005, http://www.nytimes.com/2005/11/14/opinion/14blochemarks.html?_r=1&scp=1&sq=interrogation:+doing+unto+others&oref=slogin; Lemov, *The World as Laboratory: Experiments with Mice, Mazes and Men*, pp.195-199.

[206] Lemov, "The American Science of Interrogation." The 1983 CIA Manual on Human Resource Exploitation Training, which was used by the CIA and elite military forces to train Latin American military units in the mid-1980s, indicates that coercive techniques are justified and "reserved for those subjects who have been trained or who have developed the ability to resist non-coercive techniques." Central Intelligence Agency, *Human Resources Training Manual*

(1983), sec. K-4. This manual was the subject of hearings concerning U.S. involvement in human rights abuses in Latin America. For further information, *see* "Prisoner Abuse: Patterns from the Past," National Security Archive, *National Security Archive Electronic Briefing Book No. 122* (Washington DC: George Washington University, May 12, 2004), http://www.gwu.edu/~nsarchiv/NSAEBB/NSAEBB122/index.htm.

[207] Central Intelligence Agency, *KUBARK, Counterintelligence Interrogations*, (Central Intelligence Agency, July 1965), p. 85; CIA, *Human Resources Exploitation Training Manual*, secs. F-2, K-6-7, L-3, L-4, L-5.

[208] CIA, *KUBARK,Counterintelligence Interrogations*, p. 84; Central Intelligence Agency, *Human Resources Exploitation Training Manual*, sec. L-7. The *Human Resources Exploitation Training Manual* raises under the heading, "Objections to Coercion," the view of some psychologists "that the subject's ability to recall and communicate information accurately is as impaired as his will to resist." CIA, *Human Resources Exploitation Training Manual*, sec. L-7. In addition, the KUBARK manual cautions, "direct physical brutality creates only resentment, hostility, and further defiance." CIA, *KUBARK,Counterintelligence Interrogations*, p. 91. *See also* Kleinman, "KUBARK Counterintelligence Interrogation Review: Observations of an Interrogator," pp. 128-130 (noting that despite criticism of KUBARK manual for its discussion of coercion, the manual does not characterize coercion as a "necessary" or "viable" means of obtaining reliable and useful information).

[209] Many articles describe both the similarities between techniques used in SERE training and techniques reportedly used on certain detainees, as well as evidence of ties between SERE officials and CIA and military interrogators, including tutorials on SERE techniques. *See, e.g.*, Eban, "Rorschach and Awe;" Mark Benjamin, "Torture Teachers," *Salon.com*, June 29, 2007, http://www.salon.com/news/feature/2006/06/29/torture/index_np.html; Mayer, "The Experiment;" Kleinman, "KUBARK Counterintelligence Interrogation Review: Observations of an Interrogator," pp. 97-98. As early as September 2002, military intelligence officers at Guantánamo were briefed on "techniques and methods used in resistance (to interrogation) training at SERE schools," and received further SERE training thereafter. DoD, *Review of Detainee Abuse*, pp. 25-26. Kleinman explains there are three "intractable" problems with adopting SERE techniques for the purpose of interrogating terrorism suspects. First, SERE instructors employ illegal coercive techniques in portraying enemy interrogators. Second, SERE instructors emphasize the re-creation of stressful situations as opposed to the teaching of in-depth questioning required for intelligence interrogation. Third, SERE instructors do not have the requisite language training and subject matter knowledge necessary for intelligence interrogation. Kleinman, "KUBARK Counterintelligence Interrogation Review: Observations of an Interrogator," p. 98. FBI agents at Guantánamo complained of the use of SERE tactics. One FBI document summarizing abusive interrogation issues notes: "FBI personnel assigned to the Military Tribunal effort involving GTMO detainees has during the review of discovery material seen, on a few rare occasions, documentation of SERE techniques being noted in interviews conducted by Military personnel. In these instances, the material was called to the attention of military's Criminal Investigative Task Force (CITF), and Office of Military Commissions (OMC) personnel." Federal Bureau of Investigation, "Detainee Interview (Abusive Interrogation Issues)," May 6, 2004, (on file with Human Rights First). A redacted version is available at http://www.aclu.org/torturefoia/released/FBI_4194.pdf. The same document also states that, in late 2002 and into mid-2003, the FBI's Behavioral Analysis Unit objected to U.S. military interrogation techniques, particularly the use of SERE techniques, and that the FBI's concerns were briefed to Maj. Gen. Geoffrey Miller, then-commander at Guantánamo.

[210] Dedman, "Can the '20th Hijacker' of Sept. 11 Stand Trial?"

[211] *Army Field Manual 2-22.3*, secs. 5-75, 8-18. The manual also states: "All captured or detained personnel, regardless of status, shall be treated humanely, and in accordance with the Detainee Treatment Act of 2005 and DoD Directive 2310.1E, 'Department of Defense Detainee Program,' and no person in the custody or under the control of DoD, regardless of nationality or physical location, shall be subject to torture or cruel, inhuman, or degrading treatment or punishment, in accordance with and as defined in U.S. law." *Ibid*, sec. 5-74.

[212] *Ibid*, sec. 5-74.

[213] U.S. Department of the Army, *Field Manual 34-52: Intelligence Interrogation* (Washington, DC: Department of the Army, September 1992), p. 1-8, http://www4.army.mil/ocpa/reports/ArmyIGDetaineeAbuse/FM34-52IntelInterrogation.pdf.

[214] Lt. Gen. John Kimmons, "Department of Defense News Briefing with Deputy Assistant Secretary Stimson and Lt. Gen. Kimmons from the Pentagon," U.S. Department of Defense Press Briefing, Transcript, September 6, 2006, http://www.defenselink.mil/transcripts/transcript.aspx?transcriptid=3712. *See also* Jackson Diehl, "Pistachios at Guantánamo," *Washington Post*, July 23, 2007, http://www.washingtonpost.com/wp-dyn/content/article/2007/07/22/AR2007072200882.html (quoting Guantánamo officials' views that relationship building approaches and positive incentives worked more effectively than harsh methods). The military's top lawyers have also questioned the efficacy of many of the abusive techniques authorized at Guantánamo. U.S. Navy Judge Advocate General Bruce MacDonald, for example, stated before the Senate Judiciary Committee in August 2006: "I would just offer that, having visited Guantánamo and talked to our interrogators at Guantánamo, that they strongly believe that coercion and torture doesn't work, and that it doesn't get you the actionable intelligence that we need. They're engaged in a much longer process of building trust with the detainees through fair treatment in the hopes, that as General Myers just said, of getting them to come forward with information of their own accord, and they have been successful." Rear Admiral Bruce MacDonald, Hearing in Senate Judiciary Committee, *The Authority to Prosecute Terrorists Under The War Crimes Provisions of Title 18*, 109th Cong., 2nd sess., 2006. *See also* Memorandum from Maj. Gen. Thomas J. Romig, U.S. Army, the Judge Advocate General, to General Counsel of the Department of the Air Force, "Draft Report and Recommendations of the Working Group to Assess the Legal, Policy and Operational Issues Related to Interrogation of Detainees Held by the U.S. Armed Forces in the War on Terrorism," March 3, 2003, http://www.humanrightsfirst.org/us_law/etn/pdf/jag-memos-072505.pdf ("Some of these techniques do not comport with Army doctrine as set forth in the Field Manual (FM) 34-52 Intelligence Interrogation, and may be of questionable practical value in obtaining reliable information from those being interrogated").

[215] *Intelligence Authorization Act for Fiscal Year 2008*, HR 2082, 110th Cong., 2nd sess., section 327; David M. Herszenhorn, "Bill Curbing Terror Interrogators is Sent to Bush, Who Has Vowed to Veto It," *New York Times*, February 14, 2008,

http://www.nytimes.com/2008/02/14/washington/14cong.html; President George W. Bush, President's Radio Address, March 8, 2008, http://www.whitehouse.gov/news/releases/2008/03/20080308.html.

[216] FBI e-mail from [redacted] to Gary Bald, Frankie Battle, and Arthur Cummings, "FW: Impersonating FBI at GTMO," December 5, 2003, http://www.aclu.org/torturefoia/released/FBI.121504.3977.pdf.

[217] FBI Memorandum from CIRG to Inspection, "Counterterrorism Division, GTMO, Inspection Special Inquiry," July 13, 2004.

[218] FBI e-mail from [redacted] to T.J. Harrington, "Instruction to GTMO Interrogators, May 10, 2004, http://www.senate.gov/~Levin/newsroom/supporting/2005/DOJ.032105.pdf. The agent also reported in the memo that at least some high-level officials from Guantánamo agreed that, at best, the military's coercive interrogation produced the same information that was previously elicited by the FBI through non-coercive methods (describing video telephone conference with Maj. Gen. Geoffrey Miller, FBI, CITF, [redacted] and the Pentagon Detainee Policy Committee). In response to the Abu Ghraib scandal and disclosure of the U.S. military's interrogation policy at Guantánamo, one FBI agent wrote: "The BAUs [Behavioral Analysis Units] are officially on record via ECs to FBIHQ regarding our concern about DoD interrogation techniques and our position recommending 'rapport based' doctrine regarding detainee interviews and interrogations at GTMO." FBI e-mail from [redacted] to [redacted], "GTMO Related E-mails, Notes, etc.," May 10, 2004, http://www.aclu.org/torturefoia/released/FBI_4142.pdf. Another FBI e-mail communication addresses a CNN report on Brig. Gen. Janice Karpinski's allegation that Maj. Gen. Geoffrey Miller had informed her he was going to "gitmo-ize" the Abu Ghraib prison. The e-mail states: "I am not sure what this means. However, if this refers to intell gathering as I suspect, it suggests he has continued to support interrogation strategies we not only advised against, but questioned in terms of effectiveness." FBI e-mail from [redacted] to [redacted], "Current Events," May 13, 2004, http://www.aclu.org/torturefoia/released/FBI_4140.pdf.

[219] Jack Cloonan, phone interview by Human Rights First, July 19, 2005.

[220] Jack Cloonan, interview by Frontline, October 18, 2005. Former Navy General Counsel Alberto Mora has also criticized the coercive techniques employed at Guantánamo, stating that "[t]he weight of expert opinion held that the most effective interrogation techniques to employ against individuals with the psychological profile of the al Qaeda or Taliban detainees were 'relationship-based,' that is, they relied on the mutual trust achieved in the course of developing a non-coercive relationship to break down the detainee's resistance to interrogation. Coercive interrogations....were counter-productive to the implementation of relationship-based strategies." Mora memo, p. 6, http://www.aclu.org/safefree/torture/29228res20040707.html#attach (describing Dr. Michael Gelles' analysis of the scientific and academic literature on coercive and non-coercive interrogation in a 2004 memorandum to the Navy's inspector general).

[221] Michael Gelles, "The Role of Psychologists in the Global War on Terror: Professional and Ethical Considerations," (speech at Yeshiva University Symposium, New York, NY, June 22, 2007 (notes on file with Human Rights First). See also Charlie Savage, "Split Seen on Interrogation Techniques," Boston Globe, March 31, 2005, http://www.boston.com/news/world/latinamerica/articles/2005/03/31/split_seen_on_interrogation_techniques/.

[222] Savage, "Split Seen on Interrogation Techniques," (emphasis added). See also Gelles, "The Role of Psychologists in the Global War on Terror: Professional and Ethical Considerations."

[223] A useful description of the FBI interview and interrogation process may be found in Ariel Neuman and Daniel Salinas-Serrano, "Custodial Interrogations: What We Know, What We Do, and What We Can Learn From Law Enforcement Experiences," Educing Information: Interrogation: Science and Art: Intelligence Science Board Study Report on Educing Information, Phase 1 (Washington, DC: National Defense Intelligence College Press, September 2006), pp. 198-202. Neuman and Salinas-Serrano further describe the interview and interrogation training for Federal Law Enforcement, which includes all criminal investigators other than those with the FBI, DEA and U.S. Postal Service. Ibid, pp. 202-207.

[224] Mayer, "Outsourcing Torture."

[225] Jack Cloonan, (former FBI special agent), phone interview by Human Rights First, July 19, 2005. See also Jack Cloonan, interview by Frontline, "Frontline: The Torture Question," PBS Online, October 18, 2005, http://www.pbs.org/wgbh/pages/frontline/torture/interviews/cloonan.html ("This is the type of stuff, again, that we dealt with in the usual setting that the bureau found themselves in, in ... a regular interview, because each one of these defendants, if you will, had legal representation. And those lawyers played a very vital role in gaining their subjects' cooperation with the United States government. Each one of them was seduced by our legal system that many people poke fun at, thinks cumbersome. If you could listen to these guys, and they'll tell you—I'm referring to Al Qaeda members—'You mean to tell me that the United States government will give me the legal representation?' 'Correct.' 'You mean to tell me that if I cooperate with you, that you will at least possibly protect me against retaliation?' 'Yes.' 'You mean that you could unite me with my family?' 'Yes.'").

[226] Interview with source from the Office of Military Commissions.

[227] Chief Warrant Officer 4 L.J. "Jim" Powlen, "Criminal Investigation Task Force," Military Police, PB 19-07-1, www.wood.army.mil/mpbulletin/pdfs/Spring%2007%20pdfs/Powlen.pdf; Brig. Gen. Eric Patterson, "CITF: Criminal Investigation Task Force—OSI," TIG Brief: The Inspector General, November–December 2003, http://findarticles.com/p/articles/mi_m0PAJ/is_6_55/ai_112482127. CITF's mission is to refer cases for military commission prosecutions and identify those detainees who should be released or transferred to their home countries. Patterson, "CITF: Criminal Investigation Task Force—OSI." CITF is composed of military personnel and agents from the U.S. Secret Service, FBI, Department of Homeland Security, DoD Counterintelligence Field Activity, National Security Agency and U.S. Army Intelligence Command.

[228] The U.S. Southern Command established Joint Task Force 170 to oversee and conduct interrogations of detainees at Guantánamo for the Department of Defense in support of "operation enduring freedom." A separate unit, Joint Task Force 160, was created to oversee detention operations. The two units

were eventually merged into Joint Task Force GTMO. "Guantánamo Bay–Camp X-Ray," GlobalSecurity.org, http://www.globalsecurity.org/military/facility/guantanamo-bay_x-ray.htm. Thomas Berg, who was a staff judge advocate for JTF 160 until October 2002, provides a useful description of the relationship between the two units, one that became increasingly tense as the different objectives of the two units became clear. Lt. Col. Thomas Berg, interview by *Frontline*, "Frontline: The Torture Question," PBS Online, October 18, 2005, http://www.pbs.org/wgbh/pages/frontline/torture/interviews/berg.html ("We're supposed to protect the prisoners. We're supposed to preserve their pocket trash, for example, for forensic purposes in the event anyone ever goes to trial. It's very much a law enforcement scenario. The intel people come along, and they're there to quickly exploit intelligence. They're not concerned about the forensics, whether evidence is properly preserved or chain of custody is done or any of those things, because they want quick intel, and that's it. That's what they're coming for.").

[229] Dedman, "Battle Over Tactics Raged at Gitmo," (quoting Randy Carter, chief of operations for CITF at the interrogation booths at Guantánamo: "'I told ICE—Interrogation Control Element—I do not want any of our interrogation or interviews in the same trailer as the intel collectors are. . . .We are not to partake of any of their tactics, we are not to witness any of their tactics. We can't have the foolishness from those folks in the mix.'").

[230] The techniques were divided into categories. "Category II" included, for example, stress positions, isolation, use of phobias to induce stress, removal of clothing, nudity, 20-hour interrogations and use of falsified documents or reports. "Category III" included,techniques such as, threats of death and severe pain to the prisoner and his family, exposure to cold weather, and forms of waterboarding. "Category IV" techniques included "extraordinary rendition," or as it was described in the list of proposed techniques, sending a prisoner to another country for interrogation. The FBI memorandum found that the U.S. Constitution prohibited the following techniques: "Interrogator posing as an interrogator from a foreign nation with a reputation of harsh treatment of detainees;" "Use of stress positions (such as standing) for a maximum of 4 hrs;" "Use of falsified documents or reports;" "Hooding detainee;" "Use of 20-hour interrogation segments;" "Removal of all clothing;" "Use of individual phobias (such as fear of dogs) to induce stress;" "Use of scenarios designed to convince detainee that death or severe pain is imminent for him or his family;" "Exposure to cold weather or water (with medical monitoring)"; and "Use of wet towel and dripping water to induce the misperception of drowning." FBI Memorandum from [redacted] (BAU) at Guantánamo bay, forwarded to Marion Bowman, legal counsel, FBIHQ, "Legal Analysis of Interrogation Techniques," November 27, 2002 (on file with Human Rights First).

[231] *Ibid.*

[232] Dedman, "Can '20th Hijacker' Ever Stand Trial?" *See also* Mora memo, pp. 2-9 (describing concerns and objections of NCIS staff).

[233] Dedman, "Gitmo Interrogations Spark Battle Over Tactics." Current policy requires all CITF personnel to conduct detainee interviews in compliance with Army regulations, the Detainee Treatment Act, the Geneva Conventions and standard law enforcement techniques. E-mail from Susan Leonard, Public Affairs Officer, DoD Criminal Investigative Task Force to Avi Cover, Human Rights First, June 15, 2007.

[234] Mora memo, p. 8.

[235] Mora memo, p. 8. Retired Major General Thomas Romig, U.S. Army Judge Advocate General, from 2001 to 2005, echoes the same view, stating: "There's a serious question of whether they will ever be able to legitimately prosecute those individuals. Bravin, "The Conscience of the Colonel."

[236] Jack Cloonan (former FBI special agent), phone interview by Human Rights First, March 23, 2007.

[237] E-mail from James P. Cullen (Brig. Gen. (ret.), U.S. Army Reserve Judge Advocate General's Corp), to Avi Cover, Human Rights First, April 12, 2007 (on file with Human Rights First).

[238] *Ibid.*

[239] This marked a departure from prior practice where the two agencies had generally avoided such joint interrogations. Laura Sullivan, "Some in FBI Balked at CIA Ties," *Baltimore Sun*, May 25, 2004, http://www.baltimoresun.com/news/nationworld/bal-te.journal25may25,0,7951000,full.column. Some accounts suggest that a schism between the FBI and CIA emerged as early as November 2001, with a fight over the treatment and interrogation of a senior al Qaeda operative named Ibn al-Shakh al-Libi. *See* Hirsh, Barry and Klaidman, "Interrogation: A Tortured Debate." *See also* Jack Cloonan, phone interview by Human Rights First, July 19, 2005; Mayer, "Outsourcing Torture."

[240] Sullivan, "Some in FBI Balked at CIA Ties."

[241] Robert Mueller, Senate Committee on the Judiciary, *FBI Oversight: Terrorism and Other Topics*, 108th Cong., 2nd sess., 2004, pp. 11-12. A day prior to Mueller's congressional testimony, the FBI issued a memorandum to all FBI field offices regarding the interrogation of detainees in U.S. custody. FBI General Counsel Valerie Caproni reiterated the FBI's policy prohibiting the use of force, threats, physical abuse, threats of physical abuse or severe physical conditions or inherently coercive methods in interrogations. The memorandum specifies that, "FBI personnel shall not participate in any treatment or use any interrogation technique that is in violation of these guidelines regardless of whether the co-interrogator is in compliance with his or her own guidelines." It further explains that FBI agents are required to report any knowledge or suspicion of abuse or mistreatment of detainees by non-FBI personnel to the FBI on-scene commander. Memorandum from FBI General Counsel [redacted,] John Pistole, and Valerie Caproni to All Divisions, "Treatment of Prisoners and Detainees," May 19, 2004, http://www.aclu.org/torturefoia/search/searchdetail.php?r=2878&q=.

[242] Interview with source from the Office of Military Commissions.

www.ingramcontent.com/pod-product-compliance
Lightning Source LLC
Chambersburg PA
CBHW080526030426
42337CB00023B/4647